A. E. HOUSMAN

A. E. HOUSMAN, *aet.* 67
from a drawing by Francis Dodd

A. E. HOUSMAN

A SKETCH
TOGETHER WITH A LIST OF HIS WRITINGS
AND INDEXES TO
HIS CLASSICAL PAPERS

by

A. S. F. GOW
Fellow of Trinity College
Cambridge

HASKELL HOUSE PUBLISHERS Ltd.
Publishers of Scarce Scholarly Books
NEW YORK, N. Y. 10012
1972

HASKELL HOUSE PUBLISHERS Ltd.

Publishers of Scarce Scholarly Books

280 LAFAYETTE STREET

NEW YORK. N. Y. 10012

Library of Congress Cataloging in Publication Data

Gow, Andrew Sydenham Farrar, 1886-
   A. E. Housman; a sketch together with a list of
his writings and indexes to his classical papers.

   1. Housman, Alfred Edward, 1859-1936. 2. Housman,
Alfred Edward, 1859-1936—Bibliography. 3. Housman,
Alfred Edward, 1859-1936—Concordances.
PR4809.H15G6 1972   821'.9'12   72-699
ISBN 0-8383-1423-6

Printed in the United States of America

PREFACE

When a scholar of A. E. Housman's eminence has
disposed of much of his work in periodicals, the con-
venience of scholars no less than respect for his memory
commonly demands the publication of his Collected
Papers. Housman's will, however, contains the following clause:

> I expressly desire and wish my desire to be made as widely
> known as possible that none of my writings which have appeared
> in periodical publications shall be collected and reprinted in any
> shape or form. -

This prohibition caused little surprise to his friends,
nor is its reason in doubt. Housman's publications
extend over more than half a century; and as he was no
longer prepared to endorse a good many of the opinions
expressed during that long stretch of time, he was
unwilling to see them gathered together in a form which
might seem to imply that they had his continued
approval. Still, as the title-page of his London Introductory Lecture reminds us, *nescit vox missa reverti*, and
Housman's prohibition will not prevent scholars from
wishing to know what his opinions were. I do not think
there is any lack of *pietas* in making the path easier for
them, nor should I have compiled this book unless
I had felt some assurance that Housman would not have
disapproved of it; but I would ask those who use it

to remember why they have to look for his papers in the places of their original publication, and to reflect that the earlier a paper is, the less certainly does it represent the author's mature opinion.

In the year 1925 Housman allowed me to collect from parcels in his rooms such offprints of his articles as were still available. They numbered nearly a hundred, and tempted me to compile a complete list. This list Housman himself revised, and the resulting typescript proved useful, so that in the following year, partly for that reason and partly as a compliment to Housman, three friends, Mr E. Harrison, Professor D. S. Robertson, and Mr A. F. Scholfield, joined me in printing a hundred copies of it. To keep it up to date thereafter was not difficult, for Housman sent me offprints of anything he wrote and I was in sufficiently close touch with him to know on what work he was engaged.

This list, corrected, brought up to date, and slightly rearranged, forms the second part of the present volume; and so far as his classical work is concerned I hope that it may be found substantially complete. For the section headed 'English', however, I make no such claim. In particular, it does not direct the reader to published poems which Housman did not reprint in his two volumes of poetry, nor to the first publications of those which he did, and it does not enumerate the many impressions and reprints of *A Shropshire Lad*, *Last Poems*, and his Leslie Stephen Lecture. These lists are not a bibliography in the modern sense of the word, and strict bibliographers will find much else to repre-

hend in them; but in this matter I count it sufficient
defence to say that, of the three tasks I have declined
to undertake, Housman would have regarded the first
with annoyance and the others with contempt. I sus-
pect, however, that the English list, deliberately in-
complete in these respects, is accidentally so in others.
Apart from the poetry, its contents are, with few
exceptions, by-products of the twenty-five years he
spent in Cambridge, and though Housman did not
remember, or did not direct me to, similar writings of
an earlier date, it seems unlikely that there were none.
It might therefore have been wise to omit this section
altogether, but I have not done so since some of its
contents are of considerable interest and might easily
escape the enquirer. There is, moreover, ground for
hope that its omissions are not numerous, for friends who
knew Housman during his life in London have been
unable to tell me of any casual publications of that
period, nor, though Housman commonly kept cuttings
of anything he had written in other than classical
periodicals, were any found among his papers.

In the index of passages in classical authors which
forms the bulk of the third part of the book, my aim has
been to include not only passages on which Housman
wrote notes but also those to the correction or interpretation of which his incidental comments make some
contribution. I have not, however, admitted passages
where he merely expressed in passing his agreement
or disagreement with a particular reading or interpretation. Such judgments are very numerous, especially

where he is reviewing a book or weighing the merits of one manuscript against another; and from papers of this kind in particular it is probable that no two index-makers would have drawn precisely the same selection. My tendency has been rather to include than to omit, but since the lists which precede the index are so arranged as to facilitate the enquiries of those who wish to ascertain all the opinions expressed by Housman on a particular author, I have not, in doubtful cases, expended meticulous care upon my decision. The index of subjects contains a brief, and therefore somewhat arbitrary, selection of topics which, for one reason or another, seemed to deserve separate record.

The sketch which I have prefixed to these lists and indexes requires perhaps more apology, and if any comprehensive biography were in prospect it would not have been written. But Housman the poet and Housman the scholar, though not so far apart as is sometimes supposed, at least demand of a biographer qualities widely different and seldom united. Moreover, Housman's life falls into several markedly distinct sections, and it is hard to see who could treat of them all with sufficient knowledge. In these circumstances it seemed likely that the scholars for whom the lists and indexes are intended might welcome a brief outline of his life and some account of his scholarship; and since, to borrow his own phrase, 'now begins the steady encroachment of oblivion as those who remember him are in their turn summoned away', I have not thought it impertinent to interweave with these an impression of Housman as I knew him during the last twenty-five years of his life.

Of Housman's life before he came to Cambridge I could not have written without assistance from those who knew him during that period, and assistance has been most generously given me. His brother and sister, Mr Laurence Housman and Mrs E. W. Symons, have helped me at every turn, and with them I must thank Mr A. W. Pollard and the late Canon E. W. Watson, his contemporaries at St John's College, Oxford, Mr E. W. Hulme, his senior in the Patent Office, and Professor R. W. Chambers, his pupil at University College. Among others to whom I am indebted for information I must particularly mention Mr D. J. Walters, the present Head Master of Bromsgrove School. Written sources of information are naturally scanty, but I have quoted freely from a paper by Professor Chambers, and have taken some facts from others by Mr Pollard and Mrs Symons. These are to be published in a memorial number of *The Bromsgrovian*, of which I have been allowed to see the proofs. I have also seen an appreciation of Housman's scholarship by Professor D. S. Robertson which is to appear in *The Classical Review*.

In the preparation of the book as a whole I am greatly indebted to Mr E. Harrison, Professor Robertson, and Mr A. F. Scholfield who have grudged no time or pains in assisting me. My thanks are due also to the President and Fellows of St John's College, Oxford, for leave to reproduce Mr Francis Dodd's drawing, to Messrs

Jonathan Cape Ltd. for permission to print a poem from *More Poems*, and to the staff of the University Press for the care they have taken over a troublesome piece of typography.

A. S. F. G.

CAMBRIDGE
SEPTEMBER, 1936

CONTENTS

Acknowledgement is made to Alfred A. Knopf, Inc., for permission to reproduce on pages 52 and 53 the poem which appears in MORE POEMS.

PLATES

A. E. HOUSMAN

A SKETCH

A. E. H.

b. 26 MARCH 1859   *d.* 30 APRIL 1936

1870–1877	Bromsgrove School
1877–1881	St John's College, Oxford
1882–1892	H.M. Patent Office
1892–1911	University College, London
1911–1936	Trinity College, Cambridge

LFRED EDWARD HOUSMAN was born on
26 March 1859 at the Valley House, Fock-
bury, a scattered hamlet in Worcestershire
some two miles from Bromsgrove, where his father,
Edward Housman, was in practice as a solicitor. In
1870 he was elected to a foundation scholarship at the
Grammar School of King Edward the Sixth, Bromsgrove
(as Bromsgrove School was then called), and seven
years later the school list shows him at the head of the
school, which now numbered three of his four younger
brothers among the scholars, winner of a large number
of prizes in classical subjects, English verse, French,
and, less expectedly, freehand drawing, and scholar
elect of St John's College, Oxford.

The record is that of many another able schoolboy,
and it would be as imprudent to detect the future
editor of Manilius in the winner of Lord Lyttelton's
prize for Latin Verse as to see presage of *A Shropshire
Lad* in the headmaster's prize for an English poem.
Housman himself provided more reliable evidence as
to the growth of his scholarship. He used to ascribe his
earliest interest in antiquity to J. E. Bode's *Ballads
from Herodotus*, a book now wholly forgotten but sufficiently popular in the 'fifties to reach a second edition.
No doubt this interest was fostered by Herbert Millington, who in 1873 succeeded Dr G. J. Blore as headmaster
of Bromsgrove, for Housman spoke of him as a good
teacher for a clever boy; but in his Cambridge Inaugural

3

Lecture he said that what first turned his mind to classical studies and gave him a genuine liking for Greek and Latin was the gift, at the age of seventeen, of a copy of *Sabrinae Corolla*. It was, he pointed out, an appropriate beginning, for the editor of that volume of translations and its principal contributor was Benjamin Hall Kennedy, in whose honour the Latin chair at Cambridge was founded and subsequently named. Housman did not add, but some of his audience probably thought, that it had also another appropriateness, for the speaker himself had since culled a second and much fresher garland from the shores of Severn.

The lecturer went on to speak with enthusiastic appreciation of Kennedy's most eminent pupil and the first occupant of the chair. H. A. J. Munro, he said, was the Prometheus who fetched to England new fire from the altars of Lachmann and Madvig and Ritschl, and English scholars should salute him in the words with which Rome saluted the grave of Romulus—*o pater, o genitor, o sanguen dis oriundum, tu produxisti nos intra luminis oras*. Munro's Lucretius, Horace, and Aetna were published in the 'sixties, his *Criticisms and Elucidations of Catullus* in 1878, when Housman began his second year at Oxford. Housman never saw Munro, but at St John's College he had a copy of the *Catullus*, and probably therefore of the other books also, and he spoke, in the same lecture, of his vain attempts to obtain Munro's photograph and of the patience with which Munro had answered the letters addressed to him by an unknown Oxford undergraduate. The particular studies in which Housman was afterwards to make a name had thus begun to attract his attention, if not at school, at any rate quite early in his University career, and if they were not originally inspired by Munro, they were at any rate promoted by his writings and his encouragement. There is some irony in the reflexion that if Housman had not been told at school that his English was too poor to attract a Cambridge elector, they might have been fostered by Munro's personal teaching.

By his own University it is probable that they were not much fostered. In Cambridge it was Housman's whim to stress his alien origin, to address Oxonians resident in Cambridge at their occasional reunions as 'Fellow-exiles', and to threaten suicide if the Cambridge successes in the boat-race drew level in number with those of Oxford. In a more serious mood, however, he said that Oxford left little mark upon him except in the matter of friendships formed there; and in fact it is difficult to trace in his work evidence of what Oxford taught him. The Regius Professor of Greek throughout Housman's time was Jowett, and from the single lecture of Jowett's which he attended Housman came away disgusted by the Professor's disregard for the niceties of scholarship. Of Edwin Palmer, Corpus Professor of Latin until 1878, I never heard him speak, nor of his College teachers; of Palmer's successor, Henry Nettleship, never in terms which suggested that Housman was indebted to his teaching; and Nettleship in a testimonial spoke only of his acquaintance with Housman's published work. In 1879 Housman was placed in the first class in Moderations, but he won neither the Hertford nor the Ireland nor any University prize.

There is some tradition of his having acquitted himself creditably in the scholarship examinations, but his name was never officially mentioned by the awarders[1], and I do not know him to have gone in for any prize except the Newdigate. For this he submitted in 1879 a poem on Iona produced at an all-night sitting. At the morning chapel service which followed the words 'we have toiled all the night, and have taken nothing' fell ominously on his ears, and in fact the prize went to T. M. Mac-donald, Exhibitioner of Brasenose. In 1881 he failed in Greats.

I once asked him how the examiners had achieved this feat, and he replied that they had no option. I do not think he bore them any grudge, and with two of them, Ingram Bywater and Herbert Richards, he was afterwards on friendly terms. The programme of Greats, apart from translations from and into Greek and Latin Prose, consisted of papers on Ancient History, Logic, and Moral and Political Philosophy, reinforced by others on a formidable array of prose authorities—Plato and Aristotle, Herodotus, Thucydides and Xenophon, Plutarch and Cicero, Sallust and Tacitus. Housman knew enough of ancient philosophy to express in after life a preference for Epicurean to Stoic, and for Aristippus ('who was not afraid of words') to either; and of modern philosophy to devote some derisive pages of his

[1] In the years of Housman's eligibility the Hertford was won by D. S. Margoliouth and C. A. James, the Ireland by D. S. Margoliouth, A. C. Clark, J. W. Mackail and C. A. James. In all these examinations except that for the Ireland in 1880 the names of one or more candidates beside that of the scholar were published in the award. Among those so mentioned were A. D. Godley, W. M. Lindsay and F. W. Pember.

London Introductory Lecture to Herbert Spencer; but abstract thought of this kind was distasteful to him, and ancient history he valued less for its own sake than for the light it threw on ancient literature. The authors prescribed contained much good literature, but it was not for their literary merit that they were to be studied, and, in any case, Housman's chief love was poetry. The tuition provided by St John's College seems to have been uninspiring, or at any rate it failed to inspire him with interest in this curriculum, and he rebelled, choosing rather to spend his time over the text of Propertius than to devote himself to the pursuits proper to a Greats candidate. Probably he hoped to get through on his knowledge of Greek and Latin, but, in the event, whether because he had miscalculated the knowledge required, or because he was too fastidious to do ill what he was in no position to do otherwise, or from both reasons together, he showed up no answers to many of the questions set.[1] To what career he was at this time

[1] R. Y. Tyrrell, in 'The Old School of Classics and the New. A Dialogue of the Dead' (*Fortnightly Review*, Jan. 1888, p. 57), makes Bentley, complaining of the encroachments of archaeology upon classical studies, say to Madvig: 'He told me of a certain Oxford man who has of late published some conjectures which you or I might own with pride, and who had been "ploughed" at "Greats" in classics.' The Oxford correspondent of the *Journal of Education* took up this challenge in the following month, and made the reference plainer by speaking of 'a brilliant scholar who has contributed some really cogent emendations to Aeschylus and Propertius'. Oxford, he said, had two examinations for honours in classics, one of them in linguistic scholarship, the other in ancient history and philosophy. 'The brilliant scholar in question gained a first class in the first of these examinations, as he eminently deserved; he chose, in his own discretion, to avoid the reading required for the second, and accordingly was not classed in it.' From

7

looking forward, I do not know, and perhaps he had not looked forward very far. But if he had thought of academic preferment at Oxford, he must have known that his performance in Greats would bar the way, and have renounced the idea. It would be rash, in view of what followed, to say that such a choice, if he made it, was wrong, and it may rather be that this failure was the spur which first urged his ambition to make himself a name in scholarly pursuits, but the result of his revolt was to banish him from academic life for eleven years.

In 1881, then, Housman found himself at the end of his Oxford career, but without a degree and without immediate prospects. He returned to Bromsgrove, where his family was now living, and devoted himself to such work as was necessary for the Civil Service examination. In the course of that and the following year he assisted his old headmaster in teaching the Sixth Form at Bromsgrove, where, as Millington wrote in a testimonial ten years later, he showed himself 'a thorough and sympathetic teacher warmly interested in his work and his pupils'. In 1882 he took the Civil Service examination, accepted, after declining a post in Dublin, a Higher Division Clerkship in the Patent Office, turned his back on the west country, and came to London.

For some years after his arrival he shared lodgings with an Oxford friend, M. I. Jackson, a fellow-clerk

the official point of view this seems to be a perfectly fair statement of the case.

Bentley says that his scholar 'had been *proxime accessit* for the Ireland'. This is not true of Housman, but Tyrrell may not have wished his example to be drawn too closely from a particular individual.

in the Patent Office, who is known by name to many classical students since Housman's Manilius is dedicated to him. Jackson had gone up to St John's College as a scholar at the same time as Housman, who was a year his junior, and during their fourth year the two, with A. W. Pollard, who was also a scholar of the College, had lived together in St Giles'. Jackson was a scientist and an athlete whose contempt for letters was unconcealed, and is, indeed, referred to in the dedication. For all that, he and Housman were united by a bond of friendship which was not broken when, in 1887, Jackson went to India as Principal of the Sind College, Karachi, and was extended to Jackson's four sons, one of whom was Housman's godson. Most of Jackson's life was spent abroad, and in later life the two friends met only when Jackson was at home on leave, but their correspondence was kept up until Jackson's death in British Columbia in 1923. Housman's interest in athletics was not greater than Jackson's in literature, and a photograph of the St John's College Eight owed its incongruous presence in his rooms to the fact that Jackson had rowed in it.

If certain poems in *A Shropshire Lad* are to be regarded as expressing the poet's own view of life, it would appear that Housman was unhappy in London and homesick for the country and for the friends he had left in Worcestershire, and no doubt town life was at first irksome to so eager and observant a lover of the country. He had, however, other friends in London besides Jackson, and it is not my impression that he was unhappy for long, or that he much disliked the

9

work of the Patent Office. Long afterwards, when
asked what he did there, he replied 'As little as possible,'
but I have been assured by one who was with him in
the Office that he was a very efficient public servant.
He was for a short time private secretary to the Comp-
troller, but though the letters he wrote in that capacity
were appreciated, his impatience of any alteration in his
drafts and his outspoken criticisms were not, and he
returned to the trade-mark department, where his principal duty was to scrutinise new applications and see
that the mark proposed had not been previously
registered by someone else. I have no doubt that he
executed these tasks with the punctilious accuracy of
all his work. Classical learning was of little use in
office hours, though he was once sufficiently puzzled
by a classical scene submitted for registration to enquire
of the applicant what it represented, and elicited the
information that it was the coronation procession of the
Emperor and Empress Nero. On the other hand
Housman's tastes were known and perhaps not un-
appreciated, for when he left the Office one of his
superiors presented him with a Wedgwood medallion
of Bentley, which lay on his writing desk to the end of
his life. The gesture was friendly, though it was
unfortunate that the Bentley represented should have
been not the Master of Trinity but Wedgwood's
partner Thomas Bentley.

The Patent Office, however, had this advantage that
the hours were not so long and the work not so exacting
but that Housman was left with time of his own, and
sufficiently fresh after office hours to spend at the

British Museum long and profitable evenings which presently bore fruit. His earliest paper was one on Horace, published in 1882. The reader who turns from Housman's later work to this will think it immature, and naturally it lacks something of the cogency and finality to which we have since grown accustomed; but it was an astonishing performance for a young man of twenty-three—astonishing both in its comparative maturity and in the extent to which it foreshadows what was to come. The penetrating analyses of context, the familiarity with the way a poet talks and a scribe copies are all there—even the propensity of scribes to shuffle the order of letters, of which much was to be heard thereafter—and there is at least a foretaste of his future incisiveness of style. The *Odes* and *Epodes* of Horace, owing to their familiarity and to the attention they have attracted from the greatest scholars of the past, are a highly unpromising field for conjectural emendation, and not all the proposals here made have stood the test of time. Two of them, indeed, were substantially modified by their author six years later. But Housman cherished no undue partiality for his own emendations, and he had no severer critic than himself; and it says much for the quality of his earliest work that some of it still found a place in his lectures forty years later.

The paper on Horace represents firstfruits, and for the next six years Housman published nothing except a brief note on the *Ibis*. The real harvest began in 1888, and was surprising indeed if it be recollected that all this while he was engaged in a Government Office and free only to devote spare time to research. The publications of 1888 and of the years immediately following will be found in the list of his papers under the three Greek tragedians, under Horace, Ovid, Propertius, and Miscellanea. It is not my purpose to speak of Housman's papers in detail, and I shall not attempt to appraise the worth of these, but one of them calls for a word of comment.

The paper on Propertius which fills thirty-five pages of the *Journal of Philology*, vol. XVI, contains fifteen pages of emendations set down without argument, and a commentary on the first elegy of the first book. It opens with the words 'I see no hope of completing a presentable commentary on Propertius within the next ten years', and goes on to express the hope that his emendations will be useful to scholars, and the desire to place them on record as his own before they were anticipated by others. Propertius had been Housman's first love, and probably some of the emendations which now saw the light were produced in the hours which he refused to the curriculum of Greats. It would seem, however, that he was at this time contemplating a full-dress edition of the poet. The elaborate study of Propertius's manuscripts which began to appear in 1893 was no doubt a further section of the foundations on which this edition was to be built, and at his death there was found among his papers a complete transcript of the text, with apparatus, written in the exquisitely lucid script which he employed where special accuracy was required of printers.[1] There were, however, no

---

[1] The specimen facing this page comes from the critical note to Juv. xi 148, and should be compared with that of his ordinary hand facing

scripta leguntur quae ex cod. Par. Graec. 3049 Nauplius protulit

opusc. II p. 520 : κέρασον θερμὸν εἰς τὸ μέιζον misce calidum

in maiore (maius Par.). εἰς τὸ μικρὸν ἡδέως in minore (parvum

Par.) libenter. hoc posito, quaero quid poetae acciderit, ut illa

cum posces posce Latine circumscriberet debilitaretque tali addita-

mento, quo aperte significatur parvo poculo Graeca aliave lingua

poscendum esse. respondet Buechelerus mus. Rhen. LII pp. 395 sq.

traces of a commentary, and as Housman hardly ever destroyed a manuscript, it may be regarded as certain that no more was composed than appeared in the *Journal of Philology*. In 1932 or 1933, when his work on Manilius was complete, remembering the projected commentary, I said that I wished he would write about Propertius, and he replied that he was in fact thinking of putting together some annotations. His energy, however, was beginning to fail, other subjects intervened, and the notes were never written. Of the three poets whom he edited, Juvenal was chosen for him; Lucan and Manilius certainly not chosen because they were special favourites. For he made no pretence of admiring them, wrote of the first that his vocabulary was as commonplace as his versification, and called the second a facile and frivolous poet, the brightest facet of whose genius was an eminent aptitude for doing sums in verse. Presumably he saw in these two more opportunity than in Propertius of displaying his special gifts, and more hope of approaching finality in the solution of the problems presented, but one cannot help regretting that he abandoned a great and congenial poet on whom so much time had already been lavished.

The large output of work in 1888 and the three following years was timely. In 1892 Alfred Goodwin, who had been Professor both of Greek and of Latin at University College, London, died, and it was announced that appointments would be made to chairs of both

p. 32. The somewhat dirty appearance of the paper is due to the fact that a draft was written in pencil on the intervening lines and subsequently erased.

languages. Since leaving Oxford, Housman, not without
difficulty in the Political Economy paper, had qualified
for a pass degree, and he applied for the Professorship
of Latin, adding that if the Latin chair should be
conferred on another he would ask to be considered for
that of Greek. His application, which contained the
remarkable sentence 'in 1881 I failed to obtain honours
in the Final School of Litterae Humaniores', was
accompanied by no fewer than seventeen testimonials
from scholars as far afield as Munich and Baltimore,[1]
and he was elected to the chair of his first choice. His
colleague in the chair of Greek was for two years
W. Wyse, the editor of Isaeus. Wyse was succeeded
in 1894 by J. Arthur Platt, who became and remained
until his death in 1925 a close personal friend.

It will be noted that Housman's work in the years
immediately preceding his escape from the Patent
Office had been as much on Greek poetry as on Latin,

[1] The list is not without interest. It comprises his old headmaster
H. Millington; Robinson Ellis, T. C. Snow, and T. Herbert Warren,
who had taught him at Oxford; A. W. Pollard, an old friend, who saw
a good deal of him in London and had lately persuaded him to translate
three odes from the Greek dramatists; A. W. Verrall and R. Y. Tyrrell,
who speak of him respectively as a friend and as a correspondent; and
the following who either do not betray or expressly deny any personal
acquaintance: Lewis Campbell, G. M. Edwards, B. L. Gildersleeve,
Henry Jackson, J. B. and J. E. B. Mayor, Henry Nettleship, Arthur
Palmer, J. S. Reid, and N. Wecklein. The testimonials are highly laud-
atory. Wecklein's opinion of his Greek work is quoted below; Arthur
Palmer, the most talented Latinist in the party, writes: 'Mr Housman's
position is in the very first rank of scholars and critics.' Robinson Ellis
adds: 'Personally I have always found Mr Housman an amiable and
modest man.' In view of the things Housman subsequently said of
Ellis's work it may be doubted whether he retained that opinion for
long.

and that, though he had expressed a preference for the chair of Latin, he had contemplated also that of Greek. He was once asked why, when his early work had been so impartially distributed between the two languages, he had ceased to write about Greek; his reply was 'I found that I could not attain to excellence in both'. Excellence, as Housman used the word and exhibited the quality, involved so complete a mastery of the tools of scholarship that by the side of his the work of other scholars tends to look amateurish; and that mastery demands unremitting labour. 'A scholar', he wrote in his memoir of Platt, 'who means to build himself a monument must spend much of his life in acquiring knowledge which for its own sake is not worth having and in reading books which do not in themselves deserve to be read.' And if excellence is to be judged by such standards as these, it is certainly doubtful whether one man can any longer attain to it in the two languages. Housman's candidature at University College showed already an inclination to choose Latin rather than Greek, and his appointment there clinched the matter. His choice was certainly not based on any preference for Latin poetry to Greek, and since the ruling ambition of his life was plainly 'to build himself a monument', it is not unreasonable to conjecture that, having surveyed both fields, he saw the greater opportunity in Latin. In Aeschylus at any rate—and Aeschylus was Housman's favourite Greek poet—the certainty and finality which distinguish scores of Housman's Latin emendations are hardly to be achieved. Excellence, however, is a comparative term, and there are few who

would deny the word to Housman's papers on the
tragedians. Wecklein, sixteen years Housman's senior,
and at the time rector of the Maximilians-Gymnasium
in Munich, wrote in his testimonial for the London
chair: 'Vor allem haben seine Abhandlungen zu
Aeschylos meine Bewunderung erregt. Unter seinen
Konjekturen finden sich ganz evidente Emendationen,
die ich in meinen Ausgaben des Dichters ohne Bedenken
in den Text aufgenommen habe.... Von der weiteren
wissenschaftlichen Thätigkeit des Herrn Housman
erhoffe ich mir gerade für die griechischen Tragiker
noch die schönsten Früchte.' Thirty-two years later
A. C. Pearson sent Housman a copy of his text of
Sophocles with this note: 'Will you be so good as to
accept this copy as a recognition of the debt which I owe
to your articles on Sophocles? If I ever differ from you
it is with reluctance and a consciousness that I am
probably wrong.' Pearson, who was almost Housman's
contemporary, was Regius Professor of Greek at the
time, and though he was the most modest of men, such
a tribute to what Housman had written at the age of
thirty-three is remarkable. Pearson's Sophocles was
reviewed by Wilamowitz,[1] who singled out for special
praise three emendations of which he had not known—
two Housman's, the third Platt's; and by Housman
himself in a magisterial paper which might well have
caused the uninstructed to wonder which of the two
men was professor of Greek.

Wecklein's hope for more papers on the tragedians

[1] *Deutsche Literaturzeitung*, xlv (1924) 2318 = *Kleine Schriften*,
i 463.

was not to be fulfilled. Henceforward the publication of a new papyrus sometimes tempted Housman to gather in some of the first harvest of conjecture, and papers of this kind will be found under the headings Bacchylides, Callimachus, Euripides, Menander and Pindar. He would also, from time to time, use his unrivalled knowledge of ancient astrology to correct the text of Greek astrologers, or to help the editors of Liddell and Scott. But from 1892 onwards his choice was really firm, and within the chosen field his work was almost confined to the poets from Lucretius to Juvenal.

At University College the classical teaching was entirely in the hands of the professors until 1904, when they were given a joint assistant; and it consisted for the most part of class-work and the reading of texts. This occupied about ten hours a week in actual teaching but cannot have demanded much preparation from a scholar of Housman's calibre, especially as the classes were small and the standard of knowledge not high. In describing Platt's work in London, he wrote, 'Much of the teaching he was required to give was elementary, and he seldom had pupils who possessed a native aptitude for classical studies or intended to pursue them far', and so long as he was in London Platt's pupils were also his own. Housman, however, was not discouraged by this; his application for the post had promised that, if he were successful, he would give his best endeavours to the maintenance of his duties, and Professor R. W. Chambers, who was one of his class, has borne witness that the undertaking was carried out. His criticisms of their Latin proses sometimes, it seems, reduced the women students to tears. 'But what, I think, hurt them more (Professor Chambers continues) was the fact that, having reduced Miss Brown, Miss Jones and Miss Robinson to tears, Housman professed, when he met them next week, not to know which was Miss Brown, which Miss Jones, and which Miss Robinson. When, after nineteen years of teaching, Housman left us to take the Latin chair at Cambridge, he apologised to his assembled students, past and present, for this lack of memory. A certain Dartmoor shepherd had, just at that time, attained a place in history by getting into prison and out of it. This Dartmoor shepherd knew the faces of all his sheep. Housman ruefully admitted that *he* did not. "But then," he said, "if I had remembered all your faces, I might have forgotten more important things"—not, he hastened to explain, things more important in themselves but more important to him; had he burdened his memory by the distinction between Miss Jones and Miss Robinson, he might have forgotten that between the second and fourth declension.'

In addition to his class-work, Housman was in the habit of giving, in the spring, a course of eight or nine lectures, which, when the College began to include post-graduate courses, were announced also under that head. For the first eleven years of his professorship these lectures dealt with some period of Latin literature between Ennius and Juvenal, but in the year 1904 they changed to textual criticism with special reference to Martial, and the long paper on Martial published in 1907 presumably arose out of them. In 1911 the special subject changed to Persius, and again a long paper followed two years later.

These papers, however, represent a very small proportion of his output. The early years of his professorship are marked chiefly by the papers on the MSS of Propertius to which reference has already been made, but he also edited for J. P. Postgate's *Corpus* the *Ibis*, of which he always spoke as Ovid's masterpiece, and in 1897 there followed a dazzling series of papers on the *Heroides*. These appeared as L. C. Purser was correcting the proofs of Arthur Palmer's posthumous edition of the *Heroides*, and were summarised in the preface with a note explaining that Housman's eminence as a critic required that all his emendations should be set forth in any edition of the work. In 1899 his first paper on Manilius appeared, and the edition of the first book came out four years later. Like his other classical volumes, except the two published by the Cambridge University Press, this was printed at his own expense and sold at much below cost price. He had previously published emendations in the fifth book, and added to the volume emendations in the remaining three, since he had not, at that time, decided to proceed with an edition of the whole poem. I do not know when the decision was made, but the second book did not follow until 1912, and in the interval his work on the Bodleian fragment of Juvenal had elicited from J. P. Postgate an invitation to edit the satirist for the *Corpus Poetarum Latinorum*, and this text had resulted also in a separate edition of his own, both texts appearing in 1905. For the remainder of his stay in London his output of papers continued uninterrupted, but they need no special comment here.

The year 1896 is memorable for the appearance of *A Shropshire Lad*, and the pages of his Leslie Stephen Lecture which describe the composition of poems in that volume give a fleeting glimpse of their author walking on Hampstead Heath. Poetry, however, was not the only form of literature composed by him during this period. After the death of Arthur Platt some stray papers of his were collected into a volume to which Housman wrote a preface. It contains these words:

University College London, like many other colleges, is the abode of a Minotaur. This monster does not devour youths and maidens: it consists of them, and it preys for choice on the Professors within its reach. It is called a Literary Society, and in hopes of deserving the name it exacts periodical tribute from those whom it supposes to be literate. Studious men who might be settling *Hoti*'s business and properly basing *Oun* are expected to provide amusing discourses on subjects of which they have no official knowledge and upon which they may not be entitled even to open their mouths,

and it went on to say that seven of the papers which followed had been extorted from Platt by the Society in question. The paragraph from Housman's Cambridge Inaugural Lecture which he repeated at the beginning of the Leslie Stephen Lecture expressly disclaimed the title of critic, and when he was offered the Clark Lectureship in English Literature at Trinity College, Cambridge, he replied:

I do regard myself as a connoisseur; I think I can tell good from bad in literature. But literary criticism, referring opinions tɔ principles and setting them forth so as to command assent, is a high and rare accomplishment and quite beyond me. I remember Walter Raleigh's Clark Lecture on Landor: it was unpretending, and not adorned or even polished, but I was thinking all the while that I could never have hit the nail on the head like that. And not only have I no talent for producing the genuine article, but no taste or inclination for producing a substitute. If I devoted a whole year (and it would not take less) to the composition of six lectures on literature the result would be nothing which could give me, I do not say any satisfaction, but consolation for the wasted time; and the year would be one of anxiety and depression, the more vexatious because it would be subtracted from those minute and pedantic studies in which I am fitted to excel and which give me pleasure.

But though he refused to consider himself a critic he was no less complaisant than Platt in writing papers of a more ephemeral nature, and for the University College Literary Society he produced at one time or another essays on Matthew Arnold, Burns, Campbell, Swinburne, Tennyson, the Spasmodic School, and, in a lighter vein, Erasmus Darwin. Some of these he repeated in response to similar demands from other quarters, and I have heard him read those on Burns, Swinburne and Darwin, though not in Cambridge. In their kind they were excellent; they would not have enhanced his reputation but they would not have impaired it, and it is to be regretted that he refused an invitation from the Cambridge University Press to publish them, and gave his executors instructions that they were to be destroyed.[1]

[1] The paper on Erasmus Darwin concluded with an admirable parody, and since its theme was classical (the agreement of adjective and substantive), and Housman allowed it to be printed, I have, without

A friend once expressed to Housman the hope that the paper on Swinburne might be published, and, on hearing that it was to be destroyed after his death, ventured to suggest that if Housman thought it bad he would already have destroyed it himself. 'I do not think it bad,' said Housman; 'I think it not good enough for me'; and his precautions that these papers, which he considered πάρεργα, should not survive are characteristic. The Fitzwilliam Museum used to exhibit the manuscript of a poem by him, published in a periodical but not reprinted in either volume of verse; and when he gave the museum the manuscript of *Last Poems* he retrieved and burnt the poem he wished forgotten. In giving permission for the private reprint of the London Introductory Lecture, he wrote, 'I should like to have it stated that the Council of University College, not I, had the lecture printed. I consented, because it seemed churlish to refuse'; and Professor Chambers has described the scene at the University College Union Society when Housman was giving one of its Foundation Orations. 'We noticed, as Housman went on, that he continued tearing up little bits of paper; we noticed it because such nervous fidgetiness was unlike him. When the President at the end made the usual request for the manuscript, Hous-

many qualms of conscience, included it in the list of his works. Housman explained his own parody as due to the fact that his audience, who had been studying *The Poetry of the Anti-Jacobin*, would be familiar with *The Loves of the Triangles*, and he declined a later request for leave to reprint on the ground that his skit was much inferior to that of Canning and his friends. 'Do not tell me', he added, 'that there is much more vanity than modesty in this, because I know it already.'

man replied that it had been destroyed. As the address proceeded, he had been tearing up each page of his discourse after the other.' Similarly, for reasons which I have stated in the preface to this book, he would not have his scattered papers collected into volumes; and he was anxious that his library should not survive as a whole, lest a too busy piety should gather from its margins and publish as his emendations what he elsewhere called 'the mere guesses which we all jot down in our margins simply to help us take up the thread of thought tomorrow where we drop it today'. The fact that after his Oxford days he very rarely wrote his name in a book is probably attributable to the same anxiety, which was not confined to his writings. The Library of Trinity College, Cambridge, possessed a drawing of him by Sir William Rothenstein which Housman disliked. In 1933 he obtained leave to substitute for it another drawing by the same artist and burnt the one he thought inferior. He did, it is true, leave his brother free to print poetry found among his remains, but even that permission was guarded by a proviso that poems so printed should not fall below the level of the two published volumes, and that what was not printed should be destroyed. Housman was not the first poet or scholar who has desired 'to build himself a monument', but few can have shown such anxious solicitude in selecting the stones of which it was to be composed.

Since I have spoken of Housman's evident desire to leave a name behind him, this is perhaps the place to speak of a side of his scholarship which for a time ran counter to that ambition—the severity of his controversial style which pained or shocked many people in England, and, on the Continent, delayed the recognition of his importance. Both results were inevitable, for his attacks were often savage in the extreme.

In racing back to the feet of Alschefski Messrs Buecheler and Vahlen are hampered by two grave encumbrances: they know too much Latin, and they are not sufficiently obtuse. Among their pupils are several who comprehend neither Latin nor any other language, and whom nature has prodigally endowed at birth with that hebetude of intellect which Messrs Vahlen and Buecheler, despite their assiduous and protracted efforts, have not yet succeeded in acquiring. Thus equipped, the apprentices proceed to exegetical achievements of which their masters are incapable, and which perhaps inspire those masters less with envy than with fright: indeed I imagine that Mr Buecheler, when he first perused Mr Sudhaus' edition of the Aetna, must have felt something like Sin when she gave birth to Death.

The promptness with which these scholars defend the corrupt and the ease with which they explain the inexplicable are at first sight a strange contrast to the embarrassment they suffer when the text is sound and the difficulty they find in understanding Latin. Indeed it may almost be said of them that if they are to construe a passage fluently the passage must be corrupted first. But the one phenomenon is only the result of the other. If a man is acquainted with the Latin tongue and with the speech of poets, he is abruptly warned of corruption in a Latin poet's text by finding that he can make neither head nor tail of it. But Mr Vollmer and his fellows receive no such admonitory shock; for all Latin poets, even where the text is flawless, abound in passages of which they can make neither head nor tail.

The well-known scholars whose mistakes are pilloried in the surrounding context of these tirades can hardly

be blamed if they were slow to kiss the rod and recognise
the merit of a book whose preface was couched in such
terms; nor is it surprising that Housman's reputation
should have suffered in the eyes of a good many people
who were not themselves his victims from the apparent
pleasure he took in trouncing opponents. It was a return to the controversial methods of an earlier day which
gave some scholars a lasting distaste for the reviver.

Housman himself was of course aware of this—'For
scholars to argue against me as Mr —— argues', he
once wrote, rather impishly, at the close of a controversy, 'is just the way to foster in me that arrogant
temper to which I owe my deplorable reputation', and
it can hardly be denied that he took an artistic pleasure
in plying a weapon which he wielded with extreme
address, for the artistry was studied. The ill-judged
suggestion was once made that he should stand for the
post of Public Orator at Cambridge, and, in declining it,
he wrote: 'You none of you have any notion what a slow
and barren mind I have, nor what a trouble composition
is to me (in prose, I mean: poetry is either easy or
impossible). When the job is done, it may have a certain
amount of form and finish and perhaps a false air of
ease; but there is an awful history behind it.' He was
thinking of more formal compositions, but what he
said was at least partially true even of his learned work.
The wit which flashes out here and there in his controversial writings, and blazes with sustained brilliance
through pages of the prefaces to Manilius and Juvenal,
was no spontaneous outpouring but, as was evident from
his papers, the result of careful labour.

But if Housman derived some satisfaction from pillorying scholars whose work had roused his indignation, he commonly, as he once observed, enjoyed 'the unfair advantage of being able to say disagreeable things about them without any departure from the truth', and the prime cause of his severity was the indignation, not pleasure in its expression. 'There is no rivalry,' he had said in the noble defence of learning which closed his London Introductory Lecture, 'there is no rivalry between the studies of Arts and Laws and Science but the rivalry of fellow-soldiers in striving which can most victoriously achieve the common end of all, to set back the frontier of darkness.' Scholars guilty of intellectual slovenliness or pretentiousness were traitors to that high cause and neither deserved nor received any mercy. 'A contention', he once wrote, 'founding itself upon such evidence deserves worse names than unscientific and unmethodical; it is something remote from serious disputation and even from honest enquiry', and again, elsewhere, 'Such deficiency in craftsmanship or care or sense is not distinguishable by its consequences from malice aforethought and an intent to deceive.' In particular his anger was aroused by those who professed to formulate rules for the solution of problems which of their very nature cannot be reduced to rule. Rules of criticism, he said in his Cambridge Inaugural Lecture, were framed by the benevolent for the guidance, the support, and the restraint, of three classes of persons; they were leading-strings for infants, crutches for cripples, and strait-waistcoats for maniacs; and again, in print, 'Of course

you can have hard-and-fast rules if you like, but then
you will have false rules, and they will lead you wrong.'
Each problem which confronts a critic may be unique,
and to approach it with a preconception as to its nature,
or armed with a set of rules in the hope of sparing
yourself trouble, was a dereliction of the duty required
of a scholar, whose only legitimate weapon is sheer hard
thinking. There is no more bitterly indignant passage
in all his polemics than that provoked by some imprudent
words in an address to Buecheler:

Mr Buecheler's pupils, charmed with the simplicity of the
method, and perceiving that this is a game which any fool can
play, address him as follows: 'Ihre Schüler dürfen auf dem von
Ihnen eingeschlagenen und geebneten Wege mit dem ruhigen
Vertrauen fortschreiten, dass er zur Wahrheit führt.' *Geebneten*
indeed, μέγα νήπιε Πέρση.

> τὴν μέν τοι κακότητα καὶ ἰλαδὸν ἔστιν ἑλέσθαι
> ῥηιδίως· λείη μὲν ὁδός, μάλα δ' ἐγγύθι ναίει.
> τῆς δ' ἀρετῆς ἱδρῶτα θεοὶ προπάροιθεν ἔθηκαν
> ἀθάνατοι.

When Housman publicly fitted the dunce's cap upon
the heads of fellow-professors, it was not so much for
the particular blunder which he exposed as for some
lazy habit of thought or false principle of criticism
which the blunder exemplified, and his severity reached
its height when the false principle was, as in this
instance, acclaimed by disciples or was proclaimed by
the blunderer, and sloth or heresy assumed a missionary
guise and sought for proselytes.

Frailty of understanding is in itself no proper target for scorn
and mockery: 'nihil in eo odio dignum, misericordia digna multa'.

But the unintelligent forfeit their claim to compassion when they begin to indulge in self-complacent airs, and to call themselves sane critics, meaning that they are mechanics. And when, relying upon their numbers, they pass from self-complacency to insolence, and reprove their betters for using the brains which God has not denied them, they dry up the fount of pity.

The hebetude and inattention which lead critics into blunders like this are in themselves ridiculous enough; but when they are accompanied by prattle about 'die ersten Grundsätze der historischen Kritik', and by rebukes addressed to those whose superior care and acuteness have preserved them from such blunders, the combination is insufferable.

Probably many people found a difficulty in understanding the warmth of Housman's indignation over matters such as these and thought it factitious, for, as he himself observed, the love of truth is with most people the faintest of the passions. With Housman it was the strongest, and to overlook the fact would be to misunderstand him. In private life his serenity was seldom visibly ruffled, but one occasion lives in my memory. As we sat down to dinner in Hall, he said with disgust, 'The insufferable —— has broken out again.' I guessed that he had been reading ——'s latest book, and asked if it had no redeeming features. 'Oh *no*', he answered impatiently; 'he is so ignorant—so conceited—so obtuse.' That his indignation was genuine there could be no doubt, and the margins of his books told the same story. For if his opponents disliked what he said of them in print for the public eye, they would have disliked much more what he said of them in pencil and designed only for his own. A single example will suffice, and it is one which can now hurt nobody's feelings. C. D. Beck's *Index Euripideus* claim ., impudently enough, to be *Index accuratus et copiosus verborum formularumque omnium in Euripidis tragoediis integris et deperditarum fragmentis, nec non epistolis, occurrentium.* Opposite the claim in Housman's copy are written in a large firm hand the words 'Liar and slave'.

Since, however, the severity of his criticisms has impressed itself on the mind of many who take little interest in the more constructive side of his scholarship, there are some further observations to be made upon it. In the first place the neglect and misrepresentation of Housman's earlier work by certain scholars, especially in Germany, had been little less than scandalous. Before the publication of the preface to Manilius one offender had received a scathing admonishment, and in the fifth volume, where he was free to look back upon his own career, Housman recorded some specimens of the treatment to which he had been subjected; and it is right to remember that some at any rate whom he attacked had small title to his consideration. There is, however, little on this topic elsewhere in his writings, and I do not think that personal resentment played much part in determining the tone of his polemics. Nor, again, do I think that, as is sometimes alleged, he had any special animosity against Germany or Germans. 'Patriotism', he wrote, in 1922, 'has a great name as a virtue, and in civic matters, at the present stage of the world's history, it possibly still does more good than harm; but in the sphere of intellect it is an unmitigated nuisance. I do not know which cuts the

worse figure: a German scholar encouraging his countrymen to believe that "wir Deutsche" have nothing to
learn from foreigners, or an Englishman demonstrating
the unity of Homer by sneers at "Teutonic professors",
who are supposed by his audience to have goggle eyes
behind large spectacles, and ragged moustaches satur-
ated in lager beer, and consequently to be incapable
of forming literary judgments.' No preference for
England or France deterred Housman from exposing
English and French scholars, when they deserved it,
as mercilessly as he exposed German, and a common
count against the German was their neglect of other
Germans—in particular of Lachmann, and Haupt, and
Baehrens. When a German whom Housman had often
criticised charged an English reviewer with misrepre-
senting him, Housman was on the point of intervening
in the discussion on the side of the German, and the
paper which he began but did not finish was outspoken
in indignation. If Germans outnumber, as they do, his
victims of other nationalities, it is because Germany was
much busier than other countries with Latin poetry.[1]

In the second place, however harshly Housman wrote
of other scholars, at Cambridge, at any rate, he seldom
spoke of them with severity, and the outburst recorded

---

[1] Housman's opinion of German scholarship appears from various
passages in his published works, but an extract from a letter of 1919 (to
J. S. Phillimore) may be quoted here. 'I should say that for the last
hundred years individual German scholars have been the superiors in
genius as well as learning of all scholars outside Germany except Madvig
and Cobet; and that the herd or group vices of the German school which
you particularly reprehend took their rise from Sedan and may be expected to decline after this second and greater Jena: though indeed they
have already been declining since the early years of the century.'

above was, in my experience, quite exceptional. In conversation his more usual attitude towards such offenders was a tolerant contempt which on one occasion at least framed itself in verse. A scholar, whose imagination often outran the evidence, evoked the couplet

> When ——'s roaming footsteps fieldward fare,
> Quakes for her callow young the brooding mare.

But even these mild signs of disapproval were withheld at personal encounters, where the lion would commonly lie down in perfect amity with the lamb. At meetings of the Philological Society, when others expected him to tear to pieces some flimsy and ill-considered paper, Housman's comments were usually courteous to the point of deference; and W. E. Heitland, with whom he had previously carried on an acrimonious controversy, became in Cambridge one of his principal friends.

It must further be noted that as time went on some change was observable in the style of his attacks. The old love of truth remained, and to the end he would be found reading every word of books whose insignificance must have been apparent in ten pages, and making remorseless catalogues of their shortcomings. That was in accordance with his principles of reviewing; 'I have spent most of my time in finding faults, because finding faults, if they are real and not imaginary, is the most useful sort of criticism.' There were flashes also of the old wit, but it was used with less venom and directed rather to the frailties and follies of the human mind than at the individual. In his earlier controversies he had written as though he wished to hurt his opponent; in recent years, though exceptions can be found, it was commonly not so. He seemed more merciful to those who got things wrong, because more plainly convinced of the difficulty most people find in getting them right. In an addendum to the First Book of Manilius, published twenty-seven years later, he wrote: 'I did not praise Bechert's accuracy, because accuracy is a duty and not a virtue; but if I could have foreseen the shameful carelessness of Breiter and van Wageningen I should have said with emphasis, as I do now, that he was very accurate indeed.' He composed from time to time a Latin inscription for a memorial brass in the College Chapel,[1] and forwarded the draft for one of these with the following note: 'I enclose what I have written for Taylor. I have put it with labour into capital script in the vain hope of excluding J's and U's, which the executant will nevertheless introduce wherever he thinks proper, and only half of which will be removed'. The same mistrust will be found in the preface to *Last Poems*, and led him to revise for press all reprints of his poetry; and the mischance which left a printer's error in the order of his funeral service would have seemed to Housman no more than natural. His later controversial writings, composed in this mood, are perhaps less amusing to the malicious reader, but they must certainly

[1] In Trinity College Chapel, the inscriptions for H. M. Butler, J. W. L. Glaisher, J. M. Image, R. V. Laurence, J. Prior and H. M. Taylor are by Housman; and in the University Library, an inscription for the Scott collection of Burmese books. He composed also inscriptions for the collection of Flaxman's casts at University College and for the foundation stone of the block of classrooms known as Kyteless at Bromsgrove; and I do not suppose that this list is complete.

Trinity College.
20 Jan. 1928

Dear Gow,

I enclose what I have
written for Taylor. I have put
it with labour into capital script
in the vain hope of excluding J's
and U's, which the executant will
nevertheless introduce wherever he
thinks proper, and only half of
which will be removed.

Yours sincerely

A. E. Housman.

have been less painful to those at whom they were directed. They are the writings of a man at war, as he had always been, with the ordering of the world, but at peace, or near it, with most of his fellow-men.

In December 1910 died J. E. B. Mayor, who had succeeded Munro in the Latin chair at Cambridge and had held it for thirty-eight years. Housman required some encouragement before he would stand, and his election was not inevitable, for there were Cambridge Latinists of established reputation in the field; but to the general delight, at any rate of the younger scholars of the University, who knew him principally as the author of *A Shropshire Lad* and of the two prefaces, he was appointed. On this occasion testimonials were not asked for, and as by that time Housman had applied his lash to most of the eminent living Latinists, it is perhaps as well that they were not. He did not come into residence until the following October, but his Inaugural Lecture was delivered in the Senate House to a crowded and curious audience on 9 May 1911.[1]

Its theme was that, the study of Latin being a science conversant with literature, it ought to be treated neither

---

[1] This lecture, to which reference has already been made, was never printed, not because Housman wished to suppress it, but because he was unable to verify a statement which it contained as to the text of Shelley's *Lament* of 1821. Some account of it will be found on p. 164 of R. St J. Parry's memoir of Henry Jackson, and paragraphs from it appear at the beginning of the author's Leslie Stephen Lecture and on p. lv of the second edition of his Juvenal.

like an exact science nor as itself a branch of literature. The first of these propositions was, as has already been said, a favourite; the second, which caused some dismay among the older scholars in his audience, drew pointed attention to the contrast already present in the minds of his hearers between the author of *A Shropshire Lad* and the bitter controversialist on subjects which the world in general regards as pedantic trifles. A schola., Housman said, had no more concern with the merits of the literature with which he deals than Linnaeus or Newton with the beauties of the countryside or of the starry heavens.

Housman certainly practised what he preached, and in his scholarly writings the praise and the blame are all for scribes and editors with scarce a word for the authors, but the contrast between poet and scholar, of which too much has been made, is less complete than appears. For, on the one hand, in Housman's invectives against the follies and perversities of his fellow-scholars it is not difficult to hear the voice of the Shropshire Lad turned critic; and, on the other, though he was serious in subordinating the rôle of the literary man to that of the scholar, he knew wel' and said in print, that just literary perception, congenial intimacy with one's author, and familiarity with the speech of poets were a necessary part of a critic's equipment. The point he wished to make in his Inaugural Lecture was that subjective impressions based on what is called taste are a dangerous basis on which to emend an author's text, and doubly dangerous when the author wrote a dead language and lived two thousand years ago. Textual criticism had been too much practised upon these lines, and Housman wished to establish it on a more scientific basis of observed or observable fact. The facts established, when science has done its best, art must needs step in; and the art consists in judging, within the limits prescribed by science in the preliminary enquiry, what the author said and how he said it. There is therefore a real link between the critic of Latin texts and the poet and poetry-lover. Housman's own familiarity with the poetry of various languages was intimate, nor was it confined, even outside the classics, to the great poets. His rooms were littered with volumes of minor verse, most of which he had read, and, provided it was good, remembered; and as for great poetry, no one who had heard him quote even a few lines of it could be in any doubt as to his attitude towards it. In his Leslie Stephen Lecture he described the reactions which such poetry produced in him—the shiver in the spine, constriction of the throat, goose-flesh so pronounced as to impede him in shaving. These sensations are probably familiar, but if, as I think, they were more pronounced in Housman than in most men, it is because they were the physical symptoms of a passion as strong in him as his love of truth. And it was the combination of these two passions, not either by itself, which directed his studies and made his life's work possible.

The Inaugural Lecture touched incidentally upon another point which is of importance in any estimate of Housman's own scholarship. He had spoken of the servility towards the living which led to the omission of Juvenal xv 7 from the article *aelurus* in the *Thesaurus*

Linguae Latinae, and added that it was often found in company with lack of veneration towards the dead.[1] A man whose reputation has survived had in his favour a presumption which nobody living could claim, and to study the great scholars of the past was to enjoy intercourse with superior minds; and though there was no certainty that disagreement with such men in our conceptions of scholarship or our methods of procedure was mistaken, it was a good working hypothesis, not to be abandoned until it proved untenable. The principle is not set out expressly elsewhere in his writings, but it is readily recognisable in his flashes of anger with those who had light-heartedly brushed aside the proposals made by eminent scholars of an earlier age. No scholar has been so punctilious in renouncing his own claims in favour of an earlier emendator when he found he had been anticipated, or has expended more pains in assigning emendations to their first author, and Housman's familiarity with the work of his predecessors was quite extraordinary. He would commonly answer without hesitation the minutest questions on the history of scholarship, and seemed to have read all the works even of scholars of the second rank and to retain in his memory every detail of their lives and writings. A good instance

---

[1] See his Juvenal, ed. ii, p. lv. 'I should have written less harshly', he said in a review, 'if Mr Morel had not taken measures to secure favourable reviews from his own countrymen. By duly disparaging Baehrens (in bad Latin) on his first page, and by ritual homage to Leo and Cichorius and other acceptable names, he has done his best to create a friendly atmosphere and obtain commendation irrespective of desert; and he must not be surprised if smoke ascending from domestic altars draws in a current of cold air from abroad.'

of this searching scrutiny is the emendation in Cicero's *Second Philippic*, which he restored to its author, having found it concealed in the index of Badham's edition of Plato's *Euthydemus* and *Laches*; as an instance of his retentive memory, one of his marginalia may serve. In a paper on Richard Dawes in the *Emmanuel College Magazine*, Peter Giles had mentioned his letter to Taylor discussing the value originally attached to the letter E in the Greek alphabet, and had said that modern scholars would probably think that Taylor had the best of the argument. The controversy has long since lost all importance, and it was remote from Housman's special field, but he remembered Dawes's letter, which is printed in the *Miscellanea Critica*, with sufficient clearness to pencil the correction, 'Taylor was in the right, but Dawes had the best of the argument.'

The distinction is characteristic of him, for clearly as he saw, and harshly as he pronounced sentence upon, the faults of other scholars, the sentence was always judicial, and distaste for the faults did not blind him to the merits of the author. Few scholars, for instance, have ever been spoken of more harshly than Housman speaks of Friedrich Jacob in his Manilius, or of C. M. Francken in his Lucan, yet the first is credited with 'a body of corrections not only considerable in number but often of the most arresting ingenuity and penetration' which set him next after Bentley and Scaliger in Manilian criticism, while Francken, though 'hardly a page' of his edition 'can be read without anger and disgust', is yet said to have rendered more service to his author than his most popular modern editor. It may

not be out of place to reproduce here, as an example not
only of Housman's balanced judgments but also of the
weighty and decisive language in which he expressed
them, his estimate of Arthur Palmer, whose testimonial
had helped him to the chair at University College:

Among the critics who have emended Ovid's heroides since
the time of Heinsius the first place belongs to Bentley, the second
to Palmer, and the third to Madvig: van Lennep and Merkel
may dispute for the fourth. The list of Palmer's emendations
which I should call certain or nearly so...is not indeed a long
one: it will not compare with what he effected in Propertius
or even in Bacchylides. But in Propertius, where his achievement
equalled Baehrens' and surpassed Lachmann's, there was much
more to be done; and as for Bacchylides, skimming the first
cream off a new-found author is only child's play beside gleaning
after Bentley over a stubble where Heinsius has reaped. There
is much to censure in this edition, so I begin with this tribute:
no critic of the century has purified the text so much, and no
critic but Madvig so brilliantly. And since Palmer's death was
not noticed in this *Review* I will say more. In width and in
minuteness of learning, in stability of judgment, and even in
what is now the rarest of the virtues, precision of thought, he
had superiors among his countrymen and contemporaries: in
some of these things many excelled him, some excelled him far,
and Munro excelled him far in all. But that will not disguise
from posterity and ought not to disguise from us that Palmer was
a man more singularly and eminently gifted by nature than any
English scholar since Badham and than any English Latinist
since Markland.

Then why, both at home and abroad, was he less esteemed
than many of his inferiors? Not only nor perhaps chiefly
because the classical public in England has not even yet relin-
quished that false standard of merit which it adopted after 1825,
nor because the great North-German school of the nineteenth

century has begun to decline and has not begun to find out that it is declining, but through his own fault. His talent, like that of Heinsius, resided in felicity of instinct: it did not proceed, like Madvig's, from the perfection of intellectual power. Now the class which includes Heinsius includes also Gilbert Wakefield; and Palmer's rank in the class is nearer to Wakefield than to Heinsius. His inspiration was fitful, and when it failed him he lacked the mental force and rightness which should have filled its place. His was a nimble but not a steady wit: it could ill sustain the labour of severe and continuous thinking; so he habitually shunned that labour. He had no ungovernable passion for knowing the truth about things: he kept a very blind eye for unwelcome facts and a very deaf ear for unwelcome argument, and often mistook a wish for a reason. No one could defend more stubbornly a plain corruption, or advocate more confidently an incredible conjecture, than Palmer when the fancy took him. He had much natural elegance of taste, but it was often nullified by caprice and wilfulness, so that hardly Merkel himself has proposed uncouther emendations. Moreover Palmer was not, even for his own age and country, a learned man. He read too little, and he attended too little to what he read; and with all his genius he remained to the end of his days an amateur. And these defects he crowned with an amazing and calamitous propensity to reckless assertion.

Where in this lucid and orderly perspective of scholarship Housman saw himself, it is less easy to say. A critic once wrote of him as the first scholar in Europe. 'It is not true', said Housman, 'and if it were, ——— would not know it.' I did not ask whom he counted greater, but I have no doubt that he was thinking of Wilamowitz, of whom he always spoke with high regard. It was characteristic of him to dislike comparison with those he considered his superiors. 'I wish', he said to a pupil, 'they would not compare me with Bentley; Bentley would cut up into four of me', and Mr Percy Withers has recorded[1] a conversation in which the same comparison, coming from an older man, was refused with more asperity:

> I chanced to remark that more than once in Cambridge he had been described in my hearing as the greatest scholar since Bentley. His face darkened, his whole frame grew taut, and in an angered voice he replied: 'I will not tolerate comparison with Bentley. Bentley is alone and supreme. They may compare me with Porson if they will—the comparison is not preposterous— he surpassed me in some qualities as I claim to surpass him in others.'

It is a pity that the remainder of the discussion, in which the qualities of Bentley and Porson were compared and illustrated, has perished, but it is not to be inferred that Housman claimed equality with the latter. What he did claim is set out, though without reference to other scholars, in the retrospect in which he took leave of Manilius after more than a quarter of a century's work:

> To read attentively, think correctly, omit no relevant considera- tion, and repress self-will, are not ordinary accomplishments; yet an emendator needs much besides: just literary perception, congenial intimacy with the author, experience which must have been won by study, and mother wit which he must have brought from his mother's womb.
>
> It may be asked whether I think that I myself possess this outfit, or even most of it; and if I answer yes, that will be a new example of my notorious arrogance. I had rather be arrogant than impudent. I should not have undertaken to edit Manilius

unless I had believed that I was fit for the task; and in particular
I think myself a better judge of emendation, both when to emend
and how to emend, than most others.

It is a claim which nobody conversant with his work is
likely to dispute.

Housman's publications during the last twenty-five
years of his life need no detailed commentary here.
They include editions of the four remaining books of
Manilius and an *editio minor* of the whole poem, a text
of Lucan taken up shortly after his arrival in Cambridge
and published after he had lectured on each book
separately, and a steady flow of articles on the various
Latin poets to whom in turn he directed his attention.
Among these some preoccupation with Ovid is apparent
in 1914 and the following years, and I have a recollection
of his saying that, if more evidence were available as to
the manuscripts, he would construct a text of the ama-
tory poems. His contributions to the study of Ovid,
as to that of Propertius, are substantial, but one may
regret that the *Ibis* is the only complete text of his
editing. In 1922 he published *Last Poems*, a volume of
forty-one pieces of which part had been written in
the Shropshire Lad period; and in 1933, despite his
reluctance to pose as a literary critic, he was persuaded
to give the Leslie Stephen Lecture. He chose as his
subject *The Name and Nature of Poetry*, and the lecture
was delivered in the Senate House on the twenty-second
anniversary of his Inaugural Lecture as Professor of
Latin.

The statutory duties of the Kennedy Professor required him to examine, at first every year and later in

two years out of three, for the Chancellor's Classical Medals and the University Scholarships, and this was a duty which Housman disliked, and supposed himself to discharge badly. He certainly discharged it very conscientiously, and the only criticism I have heard from fellow-examiners is that he was inclined to be severe. The other duties of the professor were somewhat vaguely defined. He was required 'as well to devote himself to research and the advancement of knowledge in his department as to give lectures in every year'. Most good scholars, as Housman said, are fonder of learning than of teaching, but he himself liked lecturing and showed no disposition to interpret the statute lightly. Except in the Lent Term of 1934, when he had obtained leave of absence for a projected visit to Egypt, which was prevented by ill-health, he lectured twice a week in all three terms of the academic year.

The subjects on which Housman lectured in Cambridge are set out elsewhere in this volume, and some fragments of the course on *The Application of Thought to Textual Criticism* may be read in the address with the same title delivered to the Classical Association. These lectures were somewhat in the style of the prefaces, and pilloried with malicious wit a succession of eminent sinners, among whom, to the scandal of some of his audience, was the late Regius Professor of Greek, Sir Richard Jebb. They stand, however, apart from his other courses, which were all upon a stated portion of some Latin poet, and in these the sallies of wit were rare, though perhaps the more effective by their unexpectedness. If one carries the mind back to Housman's lecture room, the picture which presents itself is of a neat erect figure entering the room punctually at five minutes past the hour and disposing his notes on the desk, an icy silence while some embarrassed late-comer hurried to his place, and then the level, impassive voice setting out, without enthusiasm but with an athletic spareness and precision of phrase, just so much commentary as was necessary for the interpretation of the passage under discussion. To call his lectures inspiring would perhaps be to convey the wrong impression, for they were austere both in matter and in manner, and they made a severe demand upon their audience, but certainly nobody with tastes at all akin to his own could witness that easy command of the relevant learning, that lucid exposition and dispassionate judgment, without setting before himself a new standard of scholarship. The audiences may never have been very numerous, but they usually included some senior members of the University who found time to spare from their own teaching to go on learning and knew best where to learn; and the undergraduates who sat at his feet were commonly constant and devoted. They were not exclusively the ablest classical students in Cambridge, for some of these shrank from the intellectual effort required of them and fancied themselves better employed in listening to more flowery discourses elsewhere, while among the less accomplished there were usually a few who delighted their Directors of Studies by pursuing a course to which they had been sent experimentally. Such men would perhaps have been puzzled to explain what brought them to Housman's lecture-room so regularly, but the fact is that, in the lecture-room or out, it was impossible to listen attentively to Housman for long without becoming aware that one was in contact with a mind of extraordinary distinction; and it is not only, or even chiefly, to professional scholars that such a contact is fascinating and exhilarating.

In London, Housman's teaching had been mainly in the form of class-work, and it had brought him daily into personal contact with the undergraduates. In Cambridge his contact with them was almost confined to the lecture-room, for he did no individual teaching, held no Seminar, and only once undertook the supervision of a research student. Very occasionally he would accept an invitation to a meeting of the Trinity College Classical Reading Society and spend an evening in reading some classical work with undergraduate members of the College; and now and again an undergraduate, who knew enough of him to desire further knowledge and not enough to be aware of the presumption, would call on him uninvited. On these occasions Housman would display an affability on which those who knew him better would not have counted. But it was characteristic of him to be gentle with the young, and Professor Chambers has recorded how, at the University College Literary Society, hardened warriors sometimes declined combat with him, and how he himself declined it with the raw recruit. Professor Chambers's instance of the former case is Housman's paper on Burns, which was full of witticisms at the expense of the Scotch. W. P. Ker refused the challenge with the words, 'Forgiveness is the last refuge of malignity. I will not

forgive Professor Housman.' Many years later I heard
Housman read the same paper at Eton, and at its close
a small boy with a high voice and rich Scotch accent
said 'What for d'ye so disparise the Scots?' and
Housman, not without embarrassment, turned the
question aside. So too at Cambridge, if chance brought
an undergraduate into his company, he would be at
pains to set him at his ease, would go out of his way to
compliment a young don on some paper he had published, or would treat with unexpected deference sug-
gestions made by a junior colleague in an examination.
If therefore younger students had forced themselves
upon him, I have no doubt that, whatever he felt, he
would have received them with the same kindly encouragement he had himself experienced from Munro.
In practice, owing to his eminence and his supposed
inaccessibility, few ventured, and those few were mostly
not classical scholars.

In spite, however, of the fact that most of Housman's
influence came through the lecture-room, it was strongly
felt owing to the devotion of many of his hearers, and
before he had been more than a few years in Cambridge
he may fairly be said to have founded a school. His
disciples were never many in number, nor were they, as
is the case with a professor who directs a Seminar,
pursuing subjects suggested by Housman, or even for
the most part working in the field of Latin poetry;
but they had before them Housman's principles and his
standard of excellence, to apply, if they could, in other
branches of classical teaching and research. And when,
as sometimes happened, they became dons in Cam-

bridge, they could, if they no longer went to Housman's lectures, refresh their memories of these things by attending his frequent papers at the Philological Society.

In his lectures Housman was naturally under the necessity of discussing all the problems raised by his author, and novelties of his own were but incidents in the whole. At the Philological Society, where the paper dealt only with his own solution of a difficulty, the qualities shown in his lectures had freer scope, and one commonly came away from the meeting with the feeling that so would the recording angel on the Judgment Day read his scroll, and so would faults be amended beyond appeal or dispute. All the relevant facts would be marshalled with such seeming ease that the erudition might almost escape notice (for Housman, though scrupulous in meeting any possible objection in advance, never piled up evidence beyond his immediate need), and the conclusion or emendation followed so surely upon them that the paper left nothing to debate. We might, to evade a too tedious silence, ask this question or that; serious discussion of the paper there was none, for there was nothing left to discuss. Housman, as has already been said, would not allow his achievement to be compared with Bentley's, but they had at least some characteristics in common, and the words he had himself used of his hero are too apposite to be denied a place here.

Lucida tela diei: these are the words which come into one's mind when one has halted at some stubborn perplexity of reading or interpretation, has witnessed Scaliger and Gronovius and Huetius fumble at it one after another, and then turns to Bentley and sees

Bentley strike his finger on the place and say *thou ailest here, and here.*

Housman became a member of the Cambridge Philological Society in 1889, and he had read occasional papers to it since that year, finding, no doubt, its Proceedings and Transactions a convenient place in which to dispose some part of his large output. He had in consequence acquired friends in Cambridge and sometimes visited them. It was on one of these visits, in 1909 or 1910, that I was first introduced to him, but his appearance, though later study revealed the fine lines of face and skull, was at first sight unimpressive, and beyond a memory of a somewhat silent and impassive figure, I took little away from the dinner party at which we met except a disappointing answer to the question where he spent his vacations; he went, it seemed, not to Shropshire but to Paris. In 1911 he spent a week-end with Wilfrid Scawen Blunt, who wrote in his diary, 'He does not smoke, drinks little, and would, I think, be quite silent if he were allowed to be.'[1] Housman said the description was perfectly accurate (except that so far as he could remember there was little to drink), and certainly it tallies with my memory of my own first meeting with him. In October 1911, however, Housman, on coming into residence as Kennedy Professor, was admitted to a Fellowship at Trinity College. A few days later I was myself admitted to a Fellowship at the same College, and the way to closer acquaintance lay open.

The way lay open but it was not, for all that, a very

[1] W. S. Blunt, *My Diaries*, ii 387 (26 Nov. 1911).

easy one to pursue. Chance or choice might seat one by Housman at the High Table dinner, but Housman, as he once said, 'had no small-talk', and if one had too much respect for him to serve up mere tittle-tattle, dinner was a somewhat exhausting affair. One racked one's brain for some theme worth introducing, and found it lasting only for a few sentences of conversation. In fact such anxiety was unnecessary, for Housman, aware of his weakness, liked to be talked to, at any rate at meal-times, and endured with patience and even gratitude the converse of those from whom others fled. When one chanced to meet him on more intimate occasions, he could prove himself a spirited talker, but to the end of his life he remained, in ordinary society, a little difficult by reason of his silence. He was, moreover, a newcomer to Cambridge, and slow to overcome an initial mistrust of our intentions; and though the arrogance he sometimes showed in print was absent from his speech, he was yet sufficiently aware of his own eminence to resent what might seem a liberty taken with him by others, from shyness sometimes mistaking for a liberty what was not so meant, and, again from shyness, silencing the speaker with more asperity than he intended. Later on, when time had put our respect beyond question, one could be more venturesome, hazarding a quip with some confidence that it would be recognised and returned for what it was, not mistaken for an affront. But it was not a game one played very often, and some even of those who knew him well probably never played it at all.

For to know Housman well was not, at any rate at

this time, to know him intimately. In earlier life no doubt it had been otherwise. *A Shropshire Lad* and some of the poems published after his death spoke of friendship in terms which evidently came from the heart; and, if more proof were needed, the dedication of his Manilius was unambiguous as to the warmth of the friendship between Housman and Jackson. But if in later years Housman still had intimate friends, they did not visit him in Cambridge, or at least they did not come our way, and we knew him as one of those who deliberately choose to restrict their friendships to the surface, neither giving nor asking for confidences. It was not that he was indifferent to other people. Deaths within the circle of his acquaintance moved him strongly even when they were not near the inner circle, and the barriers wherewith he surrounded himself may have been, in part, his defences against such shocks as these. The posthumous poems, however, seem to reveal a more powerful motive, for it is plain that friendship had once meant to him a whole-hearted devotion which its objects were not always able to repay in kind.

> His folly has not fellow
> Beneath the blue of day
> That gives to man or woman
> His heart and soul away,

he wrote in *A Shropshire Lad*, and I imagine that it was disappointments of this sort which caused him, later in life, to draw such ties no tighter than was necessary for the pleasures of social intercourse. Those who pushed acquaintance far enough for it to be unembarrassed by alarm on their side and by suspicion on his could hardly fail to be aware of a generous warmth of heart however sedulously concealed, but I doubt if anybody in Cambridge pushed it further than that, and to push it even so far required both time and determination. To many of those who met him casually at High Tables or on University committees he remained, as to the outside world, a figure alarming, remote, mysterious.

To see Housman at his best, therefore, it was well to meet him in a small social circle, or at the fortnightly dinners of the Family, a dining club of a dozen members to which he belonged. He liked good cheer and good wine, of which he was a connoisseur, and, responding to their tonic, would draw upon surprising stores of knowledge in unexpected fields and show himself as vivacious as any member of the party. He would illuminate the conversation with flashes of wit, heralded by a slight arching of the wrist as it lay idle on knee or table, and by a characteristic downward glance ('He was the only person I have known,' said a member of his lecture class, 'who so habitually and ominously looked down his nose'); would pour out from his accurate and retentive memory anecdote and reminiscence with a felicity and economy of language which made him an admirable raconteur; and would greet the contributions of others with bursts of silvery laughter which retained to the end of his life something boyish and infectious. Sometimes, too, in *tête-à-tête* conversation, if one chanced upon him in a favourable mood or was lucky in one's choice of theme, the barrier of reserve would be relaxed, and one would be rewarded by discourse full of information, of apposite analogy or quotation, of judgments of men, books or events, incisive, personal and sometimes prejudiced, yet supported on challenge by arguments which were never hackneyed or commonplace.

Such occasions were, however, the exception. In general he was, as has been said, inclined to silence, and he was a lonely man. That his daily constitutional should have been solitary is not surprising, for it is known from the Leslie Stephen Lecture that it was on such occasions that his poetry came to him, and it is probable also that much of his work was done by pondering problems as he walked. And when, as often, one met him taking his daily exercise in the country some miles from Cambridge, he walked with a visibly abstracted air and often failed to notice one as he passed. But he was solitary too in College, seldom visiting and seldom visited, retiring after Hall to his book-crowded unlovely rooms in Whewell's Court to work or, perhaps more often, to read poetry or detective fiction. He would lunch or dine out, and it was possible to lure him to the theatre; but it was not easy, and unless provoked he went nowhere, and he entertained very little.

All this does not sound as though Housman led a very happy life, and those familiar with his poetry would not expect it to have been otherwise. The critic in whose eyes 'high heaven and earth ail from the prime foundation', the rebel forced 'by man's bedevilment and God's' into unwilling conformity with standards which he condemned, was marked for a life of discontents, and they were reinforced by the antinomies of his mental outlook. That his desire for friendship had been overborne by fear of what friendship might hold in store, has already been suggested, and his desire for fame was similarly counterbalanced by fear of the honours which in most men would have gratified it. He was offered many, but accepted only an Honorary Fellowship at St John's College, Oxford—not, I think, because, if one attain a sufficient eminence, it is, in the long run, more distinguished to remain plain Mr Housman without honorific prefixes and suffixes, but because he mistrusted the judgment of his fellow men. 'You should be welcome to praise me', he wrote in one of the prefaces, 'if you did not praise one another'; they might have bestowed upon him this honour or that if they had not also bestowed them upon recipients whom he thought unworthy. Moreover Housman's ambition to leave behind him a name which should endure was in conflict not only with his mistrust of human judgment and with the doubt, expressed in the last volume of his Manilius, whether there would be any long posterity for classical studies, but, more fundamentally, with his view of life as a 'long fool's-errand to the grave' and with such beliefs as to the very nature of existence as make men 'fasten their hands upon their hearts'. If Housman's philosophy was sound, then the great ambition of his life was unattainable and its pursuit futile; and among all his poems there are few more perfect, none of profounder melancholy, than that in which this truth is recognised:

> Smooth between sea and land
> Is laid the yellow sand,
> And here through summer days
> The seed of Adam plays.

Here the child comes to found
His unremaining mound,
And the grown lad to score
Two names upon the shore.

Here, on the level sand,
Between the sea and land,
What shall I build or write
Against the fall of night?

Tell me of runes to grave
That hold the bursting wave,
Or bastions to design
For longer date than mine.

Shall it be Troy or Rome
I fence against the foam,
Or my own name, to stay
When I depart for aye?

Nothing: too near at hand,
Planing the figured sand.
Effacing clean and fast
Cities not built to last
And charms devised in vain,
Pours the confounding main.

In *Seven Pillars of Wisdom* is a passage in which
Lawrence, analysing his own temperament, writes:

There was my craving to be liked—so strong and nervous
that never could I open myself friendly to another. The terror
of failure in an effort so important made me shrink from trying;
besides, there was the standard; for intimacy seemed shameful
unless the other could make the perfect reply, in the same
language, after the same method, for the same reasons.

There was a craving to be famous; and a horror of being known
to like being known. Contempt for my passion for distinction

made me refuse every offered honour. I cherished my independence almost as did a Beduin, but my impotence of vision showed me my shape best in painted pictures, and the oblique overheard remarks of others best taught me my created impression. The eagerness to overhear and oversee myself was my assault upon my own inviolate citadel.

The first paragraph perhaps fits Housman more closely than the second, but more than one of his friends, as he read the passage, thought of Housman; and Housman himself, encountering it in a review, judged it sufficiently like to add in the margin 'This is me'.
    Still,

> The troubles of our proud and angry dust
>   Are from eternity, and shall not fail.
> Bear them we can, and if we can we must,

and by the time Housman reached Cambridge he had realised that

> the sons of Adam
> Are not so evil-starred
> As they are hard,

and had come to terms with troubles such as these. A man whose mind is so perfectly adapted to the difficult and delicate tasks he has chosen out for his life's work cannot be wholly unhappy, and in Cambridge Housman found, I am sure, such happiness as he was capable of. 'The University', he once wrote, 'has been very good to me, and has given me a post in which I have duties which are not disagreeable, and opportunity for studies which I enjoy and in which I can hope to do the University credit'; and again, to one who contemplated returning to academic life after long absence, '—— will never allow you the leisure which you ought to have if you are to lay out your talents properly and enter into the joy of the Lord. It is no doubt a very pleasant society, but Cambridge is not bad, even after our lamentable loss of [A.C.] Benson.' In time, too, he became aware of and pleased by the devotion of those whom I have elsewhere called his school. When the privately printed list of his writings was sent him, his reply was characteristic in tone, but it left little doubt that he was gratified. 'However deeply I may deplore the misdirection of so much energy,' he wrote, 'it is impossible not to be touched and pleased by the proof of so much kindness and friendliness.' In later years also his eminence began to be recognised abroad as well as in England. Wilamowitz would send him a compliment, or Norden write that his Lucan was considered in Germany the greatest contribution to Latin scholarship since Lachmann's Lucretius; and such compliments, as, in another field, the success of *Last Poems* and of his Leslie Stephen Lecture, gave him a pleasure which he did not disguise. Nor is it hard to discern the reason, for the excitement created by his rare literary appearances, and the respect of scholars at home and abroad, were evidence that the monument he was building had been well and truly founded, and were a foretaste of the reward for which he had worked all his life.

It was Housman's custom to spend three weeks or a month of every summer in France, choosing each year a new district, exploring it by car, and studying the architecture, the local dishes and the local wines.

Usually he flew to Paris, but in 1929, when the fifth volume of his Manilius was nearing completion, he went by train. He was asked why, and replied that the percentage of accidents was much higher in air-travel, and that, until his Manilius was complete, his life was too valuable to risk unnecessarily. It was the last important stone to be added to the monument, and when that was in position he could afford to confine himself (apart from the *editio minor*, which involved no great labour) to occasional articles, secure that his main life's work was complete, and aware also, as the preface shows, that if its full value would remain for posterity to assess, it was not unrecognised by his contemporaries. In that year too fell his seventieth birthday, and he was beginning to reveal a certain consciousness, not perhaps of failing powers, but of failing energy and vitality. The *editio minor* of Manilius, published in 1932, ended his connexion with an author who had occupied him for more than a quarter of a century, and its completion was followed by a reaction and by a long period of depression, natural and not very important in itself, but perhaps the first sign that his health, hitherto robust, was breaking down. A year or two later his heart showed definite signs of weakness. Early in 1935 these became more serious; the 'kind and foolish comrade that breathes all night for me' began to neglect his charge, and Housman, recognising from Arnold Bennett's *Clayhanger* the nature of Cheyne-Stokes respiration, was aware that his life, which, since the failure of his health, he did not wish prolonged, was drawing to its close. From a considerable illness in the spring he

recovered sufficiently to make his annua
but in the autumn his heart was so m
his doctor, who had for a long time past tri
him to change his rooms, peremptorily fo
go on climbing the numerous flights of   ...e stairs
which led to them. Housman, without otherwise inter-
rupting his normal life, lodged for some weeks in a
nursing-home while his belongings were moved into
a much more agreeable set of rooms on the ground floor
of the Great Court, where he spent the rest of the term.
The Christmas vacation saw him again in the nursing-
home, and so much worse that any idea of lecturing in
the Lent Term of 1936 seemed preposterous. However, he refused absolutely to listen to the advice of
friends, nurses, or physicians, said that lecturing was
both a duty and a pleasure, returned to College, and
in fact delivered a course of lectures on the text of
Horace, to the advantage not only of his class but also,
surprisingly, of his own health. In the vacation he
broke down again and by Easter he was desperately
ill. He rallied sufficiently to insist on lecturing again
in the Easter Term, but this time the remedy did not
work. He gave two lectures, and, on April 24, dined
with the Family, in fair spirits but obviously very ill.
On the following day his doctor persuaded him to
return to the nursing-home, and less than a week later
he was dead.

PORTRAITS

There is no painted portrait of Housman, though he appeared among the distinguished academic figures in Sir William Rothenstein's design for a memorial for members of the English Universities, exhibited at the Arts and Crafts Exhibition at Burlington House in 1916 (no. 542) but never executed. Seven drawings, however, were made of him. They are as follows.

i. By William Rothenstein 1906. Seated half-length, profile to R. National Portrait Gallery.
(*The Portrait Drawings of William Rothenstein*, no. 218. Repr.: W. Rothenstein, *Men and Memories*, ii p. 39.)

ii. By the same 1906. Head and shoulders, ¾-face to R. Destroyed; see p. 23.
(Ib. no. 219. Repr.: ib. plate xlvii.)

iii. By the same 1906. Seated half-length, profile to R. Trinity College, Cambridge.
(Ib. no. 220.)

iv. By the same 1915. Head and shoulders, profile to L. Rutherston Collection, Manchester.
(Ib. no. 403. Repr.: *Twenty-four Portraits by William Rothenstein.*)

v. By the same 1915. Head and shoulders, profile to L. Collection of Hugh Molson, Esq.
(Ib. no. 464.)

vi. By R. M. Y. Gleadowe 1926. Head, ¾-face to L. Trinity College, Cambridge.

vii. By Francis Dodd 1926. Seated ¾-length to L. St John's College, Oxford.
(Repr.: Frontispiece.)

I have not seen no. v; of the rest, no. vii, which I have reproduced, seems to me to give on the whole the best likeness of Housman during the period in which I knew him. In the background may be observed the book-piled table of his rooms in Whewell's Court, and the celestial sphere which he used for his studies in ancient astronomy.

All other drawings which I have seen, and a small medallion, appear to derive from photographs.

LECTURES

In London Housman gave only one short course of lectures in the year; his subjects are mentioned on p. 18. In Cambridge he regularly lectured twice a week, so that his courses in the Michaelmas and Lent Terms consisted of about sixteen lectures, those in the Easter Term perhaps of twelve. The subjects on which he lectured during his twenty-five years as Kennedy Professor are set out below, the letters M, L, E, denoting the term in which the course was delivered. He was apt to repeat a course at intervals of about four years, but had no precise cycle. During the last ten years he regularly repeated, in each of two academic years, a course on the special book prescribed for textual study in Part II of the Classical Tripos for those years. These lectures, as also others particularly addressed to Part II students, are distinguished in the following list by an asterisk.

*The Application of Thought to Textual Criticism	E 1913, E 1921
CATULLUS	
Some longer poems of Catullus	E 1915
61–62, 65–66, 68	E 1917
61–62, 65–66	E 1920, E 1924, E 1927, E 1930, E 1934
64	E 1919, E 1922, E 1926, E 1929, E 1932, [E 1936]
HORACE	
*carm. i–iii	L 1930, M 1930
iv	E 1914, M 1917, M 1921, M 1925, M 1931

epodes and *carm. saec.*	E 1912, M 1915, M 1919, M 1923, M 1927, L 1935
serm. i	L 1936

JUVENAL
*vii, viii. x	L 1923

LUCAN
i	L 1912, E 1925, E 1931, E 1935
ii	M 1912, M 1928
iii	L 1914
iv	L 1915
v	L 1916
vi	M 1916
vii	L 1918
viii	L 1919
ix	L 1920
ix 839–x 546	L 1921

LUCRETIUS
*v	L 1928, L 1929
vi	L 1913, L 1917, M 1920, M 1924, L 1933

MARTIAL
*Textual criticism of Martial	E 1916
*vi, vii	M 1933, M 1934
*viii, ix	L 1925

OVID
Her. i–vi	M 1929, M 1935
i–vii	L 1922
*i–x	L 1926, L 1927
vii–xii	L 1924
Met. i	M 1913, E 1918, E 1923, E 1928, E 1933

PERSIUS
	M 1911, M 1914, M 1918, M 1922, M 1926, L 1931

PLAUTUS
capt.	L 1932, M 1932

LIST OF WRITINGS

ABBREVIATIONS

A.J.P.   American Journal of Philology
Acad.   Academy
Athen.   Athenaeum
B.P.W.   Berliner Philologische Wochenschrift
C.P.P.   Cambridge Philological Society, Proceedings
C.P.T.   Cambridge Philological Society, Transactions
C.Q.   Classical Quarterly
C.R.   Classical Review
Cam. R.   Cambridge Review
J.P.   Journal of Philology
O.G.D.   Odes from the Greek Dramatists, ed. A. W. Pollard,
          London, 1890

NOTE. Square brackets are used for the titles of papers which
are not by Housman but contain matter contributed by him.

I. GREEK AND LATIN[1]

AESCHYLUS

[Aesch. Persae 677 ff.]	c.r. i (1887) 313
On certain corruptions in the Persae of Aeschylus	a.j.p. ix (1888) 317
Aesch. P.V. 488 schol.	c.r. ii (1888) 42
The Agamemnon of Aeschylus	j.p. xvi (1888) 244
Septem contra Thebas 848–860 [translation]	o.g.d. 15; The New Republic (New York) 1928 220
REVIEW	
T. G. Tucker, *The Supplices of Aeschylus*	c.r. iv (1890) 105; cf. xiv (1900) 413

ANTHOLOGIA LATINA

C.I.L. ii Suppl. 5839, Anth. Lat. Epigr. 1113	c.r. xx (1906) 114
Carm. Bucol. Einsidl. ii 34 (Anth. Lat. Ries. 726)	c.q. iv (1910) 47
Anth. Lat. Ries. 678	c.p.p. 1917 11; c.q. xii (1918) 29
An African Inscription (Anth. Lat. Epigr., Suppl. 2296)	c.r. xli (1927) 60
Disticha de Mensibus (Anth. Lat. Ries. 665)	c.q. xxvi (1932) 129

APOLLINARIS SIDONIUS

On Apollinaris Sidonius	c.r. xiv (1900) 54

ARISTOTLE

[Note on the text of the 'Αθηναίων Πολιτεία]	c.r. v (1891) 110

[1] After the year 1897 the *Journal of Philology* appeared very irregularly. The dates here given are those of the complete volume, of which the first half may have been issued a year or more earlier.

¹ Housman also contributed notes to Oxyrhynchus Papyri xv 1793, xvii 2079, 2080; and to the following papyri of other poets: Ox. Pap. xiii 1604 (Pindar), xv 1790 (Ibycus), 1794, 1796 (anonymous hexameters).

CICERO (*cont.*)
 Dimissui esse bei Cicero pro Rosc. B.P.W. 1912 1490
  Am. § 11[1]
 Ciceroniana   C.P.P. 1912 14; J.P.
              xxxii (1913) 261

 See also Miscellanea

DOROTHEUS
 Dorotheus of Sidon   c.q. ii (1908) 47
 Dorotheus again, and others c.q. v (1911) 249
 Dorotheus once more   c.q. xvii (1923) 53

DRACONTIUS
 Astrology in Dracontius c.q. iv (1910) 191

EURIPIDES
 Alcestis 962–1005 [translation] O.G.D. 109; The New
            Republic (New York)
            1928 220
 Conjectural emendations in the C.R. iv (1890) 8
  Medea
 Emendations of Euripides' C.P.P. 1890 10
  fragments
 Euripides' Antiope   Acad. 1891 259, 305
 ΑΣΤΗΡ ΣΕΙΡΙΟΣ in Euripides, I.A. C.R. xxviii (1914) 267
  6–7
 Oxyrhynchus Papyri xvii 2078 C.R. xlii (1928) 9
  [Euripides (?), Pirithous]
  See also Sophocles

 REVIEW
 I. Flagg, *Euripides' Iphigenia among* C.R. iv (1890) 160
  the Taurians

FRONTO
 Notes on Fronto   C.P.P. 1926 21

[1] Transcribed from Madvig, *Opusc.*, ed. 2, p. 735, and signed 'J. N. Madvig†'.

GERMANICUS

The Aratea of Germanicus   C.R. xiv (1900) 26

GRATTIUS

Notes on Grattius   C.Q. xxviii (1934) 127

HERODAS

Herodas ii 65–71   C.R. xxxvi (1922) 109

HORACE

Horatiana   J.P. x (1882) 187
Horatiana [1]   J.P. xvii (1888) 303
Horatiana [2]   J.P. xviii (1890) 1
Horace, Odes iv 2 49   C.R. iv (1890) 273
Horace, Odes iv 7 [translation]   The Quarto iii (1897) 95; The Trinity Magazine iii (1922) 37; More Poems no. v

Horace, Odes i 31 17–20   C.P.P. 1918 22
Horace, Epode xiii 3   C.R. xxxvii (1923) 104
See also Miscellanea

REVIEW

F. Vollmer, *Q. Horati Flacci carmina*   C.R. xxii (1908) 88

ISOCRATES

Paneg. 40   C.R. ii (1888) 42

JUVENAL

D. IVNI IVVENALIS SATVRAE: recensuit A. E. H. (*In* Corpus Poetarum Latinorum tom. ii pp. viii & 532. London, G. Bell & Sons, 1905)

D. IVNII IVVENALIS SATVRAE: editorum in usum edidit A. E. H. London, Grant Richards, 1905; 2nd edition, Cambridge, at the University Press, 1931

JUVENAL (*cont.*)

The new fragment of Juvenal	Athen. 1899 604; C.R. xiii (1899) 266; cf. C.P.P. 1899 8
The new fragment of Juvenal	C.R. xv (1901) 263
Tunica retiarii	C.R. xviii (1904) 395
The manuscripts of Juvenal	C.P.P. 1904 4
Juvenal and two of his editors	J.P. xxxiv (1918) 40
Triste profundi imperium	J.P. xxxv (1920) 201
See also Miscellanea	

REVIEWS

S. G. Owen, *A. Persi Flacci et D. Iuni Iuuenalis saturae*	C.R. xvii (1903) 389
Owen's *Persius and Juvenal.*—A caveat	C.R. xviii (1904) 227
H. L. Wilson, *D. Iuni Iuuenalis saturarum libri V*	C.R. xvii (1903) 465
A. Ratti, *Reliquie d'un antico codice delle satire di Giovenale*	C.R. xxiv (1910) 161
U. Knoche, *Die Ueberlieferung Juvenals*	C.R. xl (1926) 170
J. L. Perret, *La transmission du texte de Juvénal*	C.R. xlii (1928) 43
P. de Labriolle, *Les Satires de Juvénal*	C.R. xlvi (1932) 131, 190
N. Vianello, *D. Iunii Iuvenalis satirae*	C.R. l (1936) 26

LUCAN

M. ANNAEI LVCANI BELLI CIVILIS LIBRI DECEM: editorum in usum edidit A. E. H. Oxford, Basil Blackwell, 1926; 2nd impression (with corrections) 1927

Pharsalia nostra	C.R. xv (1901) 129
Lucan vii 460–465	C.Q. xv (1921) 172
Three new lines of Lucan? [vii 303]	C.R. xlvi (1932) 150
See also Miscellanea	

LUCAN (*cont.*)
REVIEWS

A. Bourgery, *Lucain I–V*   c.r. xli (1927) 189
A. Bourgery & M. Ponchont,   c.r. xliv (1930) 136
   Lucain VI–X

LUCILIUS
Luciliana [1]   c.q. i (1907) 53
Luciliana [2]   c.q. i (1907) 148

LUCRETIUS
Lucretiana   j.p. xxv (1897) 226
Sincerus and Lucretius iii 717   c.q. iii (1909) 63
The first editor of Lucretius   c.r. xlii (1928) 122

REVIEW

C. Bailey, *Lucreti de rerum natura*   c.r. xiv (1900) 367;
   libri sex   cf. ib. 413

MANILIUS

M. MANILII ASTRONOMICON LIBER PRIMVS: recensuit et enarravit A. E. H. London, Grant Richards, 1903

M. MANILII ASTRONOMICON LIBER SECVNDVS: recensuit et enarravit A. E. H. London, Grant Richards, 1912

M. MANILII ASTRONOMICON LIBER TERTIVS: recensuit et enarravit A. E. H. London, Grant Richards, 1916

M. MANILII ASTRONOMICON LIBER QVARTVS: recensuit et enarravit A. E. H. London, Grant Richards, 1920

M. MANILII ASTRONOMICON LIBER QVINTVS: recensuit et enarravit A. E. H. London, The Richards Press, 1930

M. MANILII ASTRONOMICA: recensuit A. E. H. (Editio minor) Cambridge, at the University Press, 1932

Emendations in the first book of   j.p. xxvi (1899) 60
   Manilius
Emendations in the fifth book of   j.p. xxvii (1901) 162
   Manilius
On Manilius i 423   c.r. xvii (1903) 343

MANILIUS (cont.)

MARTIAL

REVIEWS

MENANDER

OVID

P. OVIDI NASONIS QVI FERTVR IBIS: recensuit A. E. H. (In Corpus Poetarum Latinorum tom. i pp. xxi & 590. London, G. Bell & Sons, 1894)

OVID (cont.)

Emendations in Ovid's Metamorphoses	C.P.P. 1889 8; C.P.T. iii (1890) 140; cf. C.R. xiv (1900) 413
Ovid's Heroides [1]	C.R. xi (1897) 102
Ovid's Heroides [2]	C.R. xi (1897) 200
Ovid's Heroides [3]	C.R. xi (1897) 238
Ovid's Heroides [4]	C.R. xi (1897) 286
Ovid's Heroides [5]	C.R. xi (1897) 425
Ovid, Art. Am. i 337	C.R. xvi (1902) 442
Versus Ovidi de piscibus et feris	C.Q. i (1907) 275
Ovid, Ibis 512 and Tristia iii 6 8	C.P.P. 1914 16; C.Q. ix (1915) 31
On some passages of Ovid	C.P.P. 1915 16
Ovidiana	C.Q. x (1916) 130
Transpositions in the Ibis of Ovid	J.P. xxxiv (1918) 222
Nihil in Ovid	C.R. xxxiii (1919) 56
De nihilo	C.R. xxxiv (1920) 161
The Ibis of Ovid	J.P. xxxv (1920) 287
Attamen and Ovid, Her. i 2	C.Q. xvi (1922) 88
Ovid, Tristia iii 2 23	C.P.P. 1927 31
Phil. Woch. 1927 pp. 1434–40 [Trist. v 1]	B.P.W. 1928 127
See also Miscellanea	

REVIEWS

A. Palmer, *P. Ouidi Nasonis Heroides*	C.R. xiii (1899) 172
S. G. Owen, *P. Ouidi Nasonis Tristium libri quinque, etc.*	Cam. R. xxxvii (1915–6) 60
A. Rostagni, *Ibis*	C.R. xxxv (1921) 67
H. Bornecque & M. Prévost, *Ovide, Héroïdes*	C.R. xliii (1929) 194

PERSIUS

Persius iii 43	C.R. iii (1889) 315
Notes on Persius	C.Q. vii (1913) 12

PERSIUS *(cont.)*

Ennius in Pers. vi 9   C.R. xlviii (1934) 50
See also Juvenal, *and* Miscellanea

PHAEDRUS

Notes on Phaedrus   C.R. xx (1906) 257

REVIEW

J. P. Postgate, *Phaedri Fabulae*   C.R. xxxiv (1920) 121
Aesopiae

PINDAR

The Paeans of Pindar   C.R. xxii (1908) 8
Vurtheimianum[1]   C.R. xxx (1916) 128

PRIAPEA

Mergere and Priap. 65   C.R. xxix (1915) 173

PROPERTIUS

Emendationes Propertianae   J.P. xvi (1888) 1, 291
The manuscripts of Propertius [1]   J.P. xxi (1893) 101
The manuscripts of Propertius [2]   J.P. xxi (1893) 161
The manuscripts of Propertius [3]   J.P. xxii (1894) 84
The manuscripts of Propertius   C.R. ix (1895) 19
A transposition in Propertius   C.Q. viii (1914) 151

REVIEWS

J. P. Postgate, *Sexti Properti car-*   C.R. ix (1895) 350
mina

S. G. Tremenheere, *The Cynthia of*   C.R. xiv (1900) 232
Propertius, done into English verse

H. E. Butler, *Sexti Properti opera*   C.R. xix (1905) 317
omnia

C. Hosius, *Sex. Propertii Elegiarum*   C.R. xxxvii (1923) 120
libri IV

H. E. Butler & E. A. Barber, *The*   C.R. xlviii (1934) 136
Elegies of Propertius

[1] Signed 'D. Erasmus'.

SENECA

Notes on Seneca's Tragedies — c.p.p. 1923 3; c.q. xvii (1923) 163

SOPHOCLES

Soph., El. 564, and Eur., I.T. 15 and 35 — c.r. i (1887) 240

Oedipus Coloneus 1211–1248 [translation] — o.g.d. 85; The New Republic (New York) 1928 220

Sophoclea — j.p. xx (1892) 25

The Oedipus Coloneus of Sophocles — a.j.p. xiii (1892) 139

Soph., O. C. 527 — c.r. vii (1893) 449

REVIEW

A. C. Pearson, *Sophoclis fabulae* — c.r. xxxix (1925) 76, 214

STATIUS

The Silvae of Statius — c.r. xx (1906) 37

A supposed anomaly of scansion in Statius — c.p.p. 1911 12

Statius, Silvae ii 7 73 — c.p.p. 1916 16

Notes on the Thebais of Statius [1] — c.q. xxvii (1933) 1

Notes on the Thebais of Statius [2] — c.q. xxvii (1933) 65

VIRGIL

Virgil, Aen. i 393–400 — c.p.p. 1892 6; c.p.t. iii (1894) 239

Virgil and Calpurnius — c.r. xvi (1902) 281

Remarks on the Culex — c.r. xvi (1902) 339

Remarks on the Ciris — c.r. xvii (1903) 303

Virgil, Aen. iv 225 — c.r. xix (1905) 260

The apparatus criticus of the Culex — c.p.t. vi (1908) 1; cf. c.p.p. 1908 7

See also Miscellanea

VIRGIL (*cont.*)

REVIEWS

G. Némethy, *Ciris epyllion pseudo-*   C.R. xxiii (1909) 224
vergilianum

W. Morel, *Poetae Latini Minores I*   C.R. xliv (1930) 234
(*Appendix Vergiliana*)

MISCELLANEA

GENERAL

Introductory Lecture delivered before the Faculties of Arts and Laws and of Science in University College, London, October 3, 1892[1]	Cambridge, at the University Press, 1892. Privately printed at the same press for John Carter and John Sparrow, 1933
On the Application of Thought to Textual Criticism	Class. Assoc. Proc. xviii (1922) 67
Prosody and Method [I]	C.Q. xxi (1927) 1
Prosody and Method II	C.Q. xxii (1928) 1

CRITICAL AND EXEGETICAL

ΣΩΦΡΟΝΗ	C.R. ii (1888) 242
Notes on Latin Poets [Pers. Mart. Juv.]	C.R. iii (1889) 199
Notes on Latin Poets [Cat. Hor. Ov.]	C.R. iv (1890) 340
Remarks on the Vatican Glossary 3321	J.P. xx (1892) 49
Elucidations of Latin Poets [Juv.]	C.R. xiii (1899) 432
Elucidations of Latin Poets [Virg.]	C.R. xiv (1900) 257
Elucidations of Latin Poets [Hor.]	C.R. xv (1901) 404

[1] This was not Housman's inaugural lecture as professor but an annual lecture introductory to the session, the delivery of which, in 1892, fell to him as junior professor. Its theme is that learning, literary and scientific alike, is desirable for its own sake. I have placed it here since it is a professorial utterance and contains a defence of classical studies, but it might not less suitably be included in the English section.

MISCELLANEA (*cont.*)

Oxyrhynchus Papyri iii 464 [Astrological epigrams]	C.R. xvii (1903) 385
The Thyestes of Varius	C.Q. xi (1917) 42
Jests of Plautus, Cicero, and Trimalchio	C.R. xxxii (1918) 162
Not Livy	Times, Sept. 22, 23, 1924
The Michigan Astrological Papyrus	Classical Philology xxii (1927) 257
The Latin for Ass	C.Q. xxiv (1930) 11; cf. C.P.P. 1929 10
Praefanda[1]	Hermes lxvi (1931) 402
Fragmenta Poetarum	C.R. xlix (1935) 166

LEXICOGRAPHICAL AND ORTHOGRAPHICAL

Adversaria orthographica	C.R. v (1891) 293
Vester = *tuus*	C.Q. iii (1909) 244
Greek Nouns in Latin Poetry from Lucretius to Juvenal	J.P. xxxi (1910) 236
ΔΙΟΣ and ΕΙΟΣ in Latin Poetry	J.P. xxxiii (1914) 54
[*Securicella*]	C.P.P. 1916 12
Siparum and *Supparus*	C.Q. xiii (1919) 149
Allobroga	C.R. xxxvii (1923) 60
Syracusius	C.P.P. 1927 31

PARODIES

Fragment of a Greek Tragedy	Bromsgrovian ii (1883) 107; University College Gazette i (1897) 100; Cornhill Magazine n.s. x (1901) 443; Trinity Magazine ii (1921) 35; privately printed at The Snail's Pace Press, Amherst,

[1] This paper was set up in type for publication in C.Q., and Housman gave copies of the proof-sheets to various friends.

76

MISCELLANEA (*cont.*)

U.S.A., 1925; Yale Review xvii (1928) 414; Apes and Parrots; ed. J. C. Squire (London, 1928) 217; New York Herald-Tribune June 14, 1936[1]

Extract from a Didactic Poem on Latin Grammar[2]

University College Gazette ii (1899) 34

LATIN VERSE

Hendecasyllables[3]

Bromsgrovian i (1882) 92

REVIEWS

W. J. Stone, *On the Use of Classical metres in English*

C.R. xiii (1899) 317

J. P. Postgate, *Corpus Poetarum Latinorum*, fasc. iii

C.R. xiv (1900) 465

[1] The text of this parody was considerably altered before its second, and again before its third appearance. The *Cornhill* text appears in *Apes and Parrots* and in the *New York Herald-Tribune*. The *Trinity Magazine* makes acknowledgements to the *Cornhill* but contains improvements in ll. 8 and 59 and differs in punctuation. The *Yale Review* speaks of recent changes by the author, but its text, apart from misprints in ll. 10 and 58, differs from that of the *Trinity Magazine* only in reverting to the punctuation of the *Cornhill*. The Amherst pamphlet, of which 92 copies were printed for Professor F. H. Fobes, I have not seen. An article in the *New York Herald-Tribune* of 7 June 1936 states that a manuscript dated 1882 was sold at Sotheby's in 1929 and was subsequently destroyed by Housman; also that there is a holograph manuscript in an American private collection. I seem to remember that this was given by Housman in exchange for the MS. of the unrevised version.

[2] See p. 21.

[3] This and the elegiac dedication of the Manilius are the only Greek or Latin verses of Housman's I have seen, though versions initialled by A. E. Haigh are sometimes ascribed to him. I have referred to his interest in *Sabrinae Corolla* (p. 4); and in the Cambridge Inaugural Lecture he defended verse-writing as being, unlike most forms of learning, an act of creation, and thereby enlivening and developing the faculties; but he had little taste for it himself.

II. ENGLISH

VERSE[1]

A SHROPSHIRE LAD	London, Kegan Paul, Trench, Trübner and Co., 1896
LAST POEMS	London, Grant Richards, Ltd., 1922
MORE POEMS [2]	London, Jonathan Cape, Ltd., 1936
Three Poems: The Parallelogram, The Amphisbaena, The Crocodile [reprinted from the Union Magazine]	Privately printed in the Department of English at University College, London, 1935

CRITICISM

THE NAME AND NATURE OF POETRY. The Leslie Stephen Lecture, delivered at Cambridge, 9 May 1933	Cambridge, at the University Press, 1933
Notes on English Literature[3]	C.P.P. 1921 16
Keats' Fall of Hyperion l. 97	Times Lit. Suppl. 1924 286
Shelley's Skylark	Times Lit. Suppl. 1928 1011

---

[1] The manuscript of *A Shropshire Lad* (lacking no. xxxv) is in the library of Trinity College, that of *Last Poems* in the Fitzwilliam Museum, Cambridge. These are the printer's 'copy'. The British Museum has another manuscript of nos. xii, xxxiii and xxxv in *Last Poems*.

[2] Published by Mr Laurence Housman after the author's death. See p. 23.

[3] This paper contains emendations in Byron, *Letters and Journals*, vi 1042 (Prothero), Rossetti, *The Orchard Pit*, Stevenson, *Letter to Henry James*, 17 June 1893; and notes on Dryden, *Poem upon the death of his late highness, Oliver*, Shelley, *I arise from dreams of thee*.

BIOGRAPHY

Obituary notice of J. M. Image	Cam. R. xli (1919–20) 112
Obituary notice of Arthur Platt	C.R. xxxix (1925) 49
Preface to NINE ESSAYS by Arthur Platt	Cambridge, at the University Press, 1927
[Obituary notice of W. T. Vesey]	The Caian xliii (1935) 92

ADDRESSES[1]

From the Fellows of Trinity College to H. M. Butler	Privately printed 1913
From the Fellows of Trinity College to Henry Jackson	Privately printed 1919
From Cambridge University to His Majesty the King [on the death of Queen Alexandra]	Cam. Univ. Reporter 1925–6 442
From Cambridge University to His Majesty the King [on the completion of the 25th year of his reign]	Cam. Univ. Reporter 1934–5 914

MISCELLANEOUS

A Morning with the Royal Family[2]	Bromsgrovian i (1882) 27, 52
Chamberlain's Maiden Speech	Times Nov. 25, 1932
Dr Fraenkel's Appointment [to the Corpus Professorship at Oxford]	Sunday Times Dec. 23, 1934

REVIEWS

The Cambridge History of English Literature, vol. xi	Cam. R. xxxvi (1914–5) 160
The Cambridge History of English Literature, vols. xiii, xiv	Cam. R. xxxviii (1916–7) 358
F. A. Simpson, Louis Napoleon and the Recovery of France	Cam. R. xliv (1922–3) 379

[1] I have seen a draft in Housman's hand for a Latin address from University College to the University of Sydney, and I suppose that as Professor of Latin at University College he may have been called upon for other such addresses.

[2] Printed without permission.

INDEXES
TO THE
CLASSICAL PAPERS

I. PASSAGES IN GREEK AND LATIN AUTHORS[1]

AESCHYLUS[2]

Prom.	488 [472] schol.	C.R. ii 42	
sept.	597 f. [610]	J.P. xvi 256	
	930 [948]	ib.	276
Pers.	145–149 [142–146]	A.J.P. ix 317	
	162–167 [159–164]	ib.	318
	165 [162]	J.P. xvi 261	
	271–280 [268–277]	A.J.P. ix 319	
	293–295 [290–292]	ib.	320
	453–456 [450–453]	ib.	321
	668–671 [665–668]	ib.	322
	677–682 [674–680]	C.R. i 313	
	815–817 [813–815]	A.J.P. ix 322	
	831 f. [829]	C.R. ii 243	
	847–853 [845–851]	A.J.P. ix 324	
Ag.	4–7	J.P. xvi 245	
	17	ib.	244
	49–59	ib.	246
	97–103	ib.	250
	104 f.	ib.	258
	110–114 [108–112]	ib.	252
	131–135 [126–130]	ib.	251
	189–193 [179–183]	C.R. ii 243	
	204 [194]	J.P. xvi 290	

[1] In these indexes no references are given to abstracts of papers subsequently published in full, nor do they include matters discussed in Housman's Juvenal, Lucan and Manilius. Where two or more references to a single passage or subject are given, they are arranged as far as possible in chronological order.

[2] Wecklein's numeration; Dindorf's added in brackets where divergent.

AESCHYLUS (*cont.*)

Ag.	207 [197]	J.P. xvi	290
	413–444 [403–436]	ib.	254
	498–504 [493–499]	ib.	264
	550–552 [545–547]	ib.	266
	560–563 [555–558]	ib.	266
	589 [584]	C.R. ii	244
	723 [722]	J.P. xvi	248
	796 [805]	ib.	257
	886–894 [895–903]	ib.	269
	990–1009 [1001–1024]	ib.	271
	1083f. [1098]	ib.	256
	1205 [1206]	ib.	278
	1321–1325 [1322–1326]	ib.	278
	1432f. [1431]	ib.	268
	1456–1458 [1455–1457]	ib.	281
	1476–1485 [1475–1484]	ib.	282
	1531 [1529]	ib.	283
	1537f. [1535]	ib.	279
	1567–1576 [1568–1576]	ib.	277
	1578f.	ib.	286
	1590–1597	ib.	284
	1654–1665	ib.	286
Cho.	124	A.J.P. xiii	150
	779–782 [783–786]	C.R. ii	244
Eum.	803 [800]	A.J.P. ix	322

AETNA

See Virgil

ANTHOLOGIA LATINA (Riese)

See also Dracontius

439	I	[P.L.M. iv 76]	C.Q. xxi	3
458		[P.L.M. iv 83]	ib.	7
486	157	[P.L.M. v 71]	C.Q. xxviii	129
665		[P.L.M. i 210]	C.Q. xxvi	129

84

ANTHOLOGIA LATINA *(cont.)*

678	[P.L.M. v 350]	c.q. xii 29
726 27–34	[P.L.M. iii 63]	c.q. iv 47
761 2	[P.L.M. v 380]	c.q. xii 32
798	[P.L.M. v 382]	ib. 36

ANTHOLOGIA LATINA EPIGRAPHICA (Buecheler)

45	Hermes lxvi 406
331 16	c.r. xv 155
1113	c.r. xx 114

—— Suppl. (Lommatzsch)

2041	c.r. xli 61
2062	ib. 61
2292	ib. 61
2296	ib. 60

ANTIOCHUS.
See Catalogus codicum astrologorum

APOLLINARIS SIDONIUS

ep. ii 2 2	c.r. xiv 54
vi 8 2	ib. 54

APOLLONIUS RHODIUS

iv 321	c.q. x 136

APPULEIUS

Asclep. 21	Hermes lxvi 412

ARISTOTLE

Ath. Pol. 13	c.r. v 110

AVIENUS

passim	c.r. xvi 103
136 f.	c.r. xiv 34
164	ib. 30
187	ib. 27

BACCHYLIDES

passim	c.r. xii 68
v 8–16	ib. 216
129	ib. 216
184	ib. 216
vii 10 f.	ib. 140
ix 39	c.r. xx 115
45 f.	c.r. xii 140
xi 26	c.r. xx 115
118–120	c.r. xii 216
xiii 61	ib. 140
67	ib. 140
96	ib. 140
97	ib. 217
153	c.r. xxii 12
xiv 1–7	c.r. xii 217
xvii passim	ib. 134, 217
119	c.r. xx 115

CALLIMACHUS

epigr. 54	c.q. iv 120
fr. 9 Pfeiffer, passim	ib. 114

CALPURNIUS

v 32–35	c.r. xvi 282

CATALOGUS CODICUM ASTROLOGORUM

i 108–113 (Antiochus)	c.q. ii 51, 62
v pt 3 49 f. (Dorotheus)	c.q. v 250
96	ib. 250
111	ib. 251
122 (Dorotheus)	ib. 249
125 ,,	ib. 249
vi 67 ,,	c.q. ii 47
91–113 ,,	ib. 47
viii pt 4 221–224 ,,	c.q. xvii 53

CICERO (*cont.*)
ad Att. ii 19 4	J.P. xxxii 263
xiv 10 1	ib. 263
ad Q. frat. ii 9 3	C.Q. xiii 72
10 1	C.R. xvi 443

COLUMELLA
x 262	C.R. xx 40

CORPUS GLOSSARIORUM LATINORUM
[iv] Vat. 3321 passim	J.P. xx 49
v 655 f. [Par. 7730]	C.R. xxxvii 61

DOROTHEUS
See Catalogus codicum astrologorum

DRACONTIUS
de mens. 13 f.	C.Q. iv 192
Medea 396–403	ib. 193
Orestes 462–470	ib. 194

ENNIUS
ann. 16 Vahlen [483 Mueller]	C.R. xlviii 50
148 [149]	C.Q. xxi 11
301 [339]	C.R. xlix 166
Androm. aechm. 120 [171]	C.Q. ix 230

ETYMOLOGICUM MAGNUM
434 15	J.P. xxxv 301

EURIPIDES
Med. 24–26	C.R. iv 10
119–130	ib. 8
319 f.	ib. 10
339	ib. 10
351–356	ib. 10
381–383	ib. 10
734–740	ib. 10

EURIPIDES *(cont.)*

Med.	856–859	C.R. iv 11
	1317	ib. 11
Hipp.	1032–1035	C.R. ii 243
Andr.	197	J.P. xvi 275
Herc.	1351	C.R. xvii 310
Tro.	990f.	C.R. ii 245
	1055–1057	ib. 243
I.T.	15	C.R. i 240
	35	ib. 240
	414	J.P. xvi 276
	740	C.P.P. 1890 11
	755–758	A.J.P. ix 325
Bacch.	188	J.P. xx 26
	1302	C.R. ii 245
I.A.	6f.	C.R. xxviii 267
	1431	C.R. ii 245
fr.	166 Nauck²	A.J.P. xiii 160
	235	C.P.P. 1890 10
	298	ib. 11
	299	J.P. xx 27
	330	C.P.P. 1890 11
	495	ib. 11
	550	J.P. xvi 270
	793	C.P.P. 1890 11
	860	ib. 11
	897	ib. 11
	996	ib. 11
	1088	ib. 11
	Antiope	Acad. 1891 259, 305
Eur. (?)	*Pirithous*	C.R. xlii 9

FRAGMENTA POETARUM LATINORUM (Morel)
See also Ennius, Lucilius, Ovid

Q. Cicero	C.R. xlii 78

GREEK ASTROLOGICAL TREATISES
Comm. Ptol. *tetr.* (ed. Basil. 1559)   C.Q. iv 193
   p. 77
   See also Papyri

HERODAS
   ii 65–71   C.R. xxxvi 109

HERODIAN
   i 136 18 Lentz   J.P. xxxiii 58
   ii 230 28   ib.   58
      424 4   ib.   58

HESYCHIUS
   s.v. ἀνετῶς   C.Q. iv 117

HORACE
   archetype of mss   J.P. xvii 308
   carm. i 6   13–16   ib.   303
          12 31   ib.   308
              33–40   ib.   305
          16 6   J.P. xviii 10
          31 17–20   C.P.P. 1918 22
          34 5–8   C.R. xvi 445
       ii 2   1–4   J.P. x 187; xvii 309
          3   1–4   C.R. iv 341
          5   13–15   J.P. xviii 10
          18 14   C.R. xx 257
              32–40   J.P. xvii 310
      iii 4   9–13   ib.   313
              50   C.P.T. iii 146
          5   31–40   J.P. x 188; xvii 314
          7   20   J.P. xvi 26
          11 15–20   J.P. x 189
          26 1–8   ib. 190
       iv 2   49   C.R. iv 273
          4   65–68   J.P. x 191

HORACE (*cont.*)

carm. iv 6	13–20	J.P. xvii 316
7	15	C.R. v 295
10	2	J.P. xviii 18
12	5–8	J.P. x 191
13	17–22	J.P. xvii 317
epod. 1	7–14	J.P. x 192
2	37	J.P. xviii 17
8	15–18	J.P. xvii 318
9	passim	J.P. x 193
13	3	C.R. xxxvii 104
	11–14	J.P. xvii 319
15	1–10	C.R. xv 404
16	12	C.R. v 295
serm. i 1	29	J.P. xviii 14
2	77–82	ib. 1
3	38–42	ib. 3
	99–105	ib. 5
	117–124	ib. 8
4	100–103	ib. 10
6	100–104	ib. 12
8	33–36	ib. 12
ii 2	11–13	C.R. xv 405
	123–125	J.P. xviii 15
3	172	C.R. v 296
	208	C.R. iv 273
6	28–31	J.P. xviii 19
8	15	C.Q. vii 28
epist. i 1	53–60	J.P. xviii 20
2	27–33	ib. 21
5	8–11	ib. 23
6	40	J.P. xxxi 265
ii 2	87–90	J.P. xviii 24
a.p.	60–63	ib. 26
	101–104	ib. 29

HORACE (*cont.*)
a.p.   354–360 ..... J.P. xviii 32
         391–401 ..... ib.   30
         395 ..... J.P. xvi 24
         431–437 ..... J.P. xviii 34

HYGINUS
   113 ..... C.R. xi 103

ILIAS LATINA
   628 ..... J.P. xxxi 246

ISOCRATES
paneg. 40 ..... C.R. ii 42

JUVENAL
   mss of ..... C.R. xvii 390; C.P.P.
1904 4; C.R. xxiv 161;
xl 170; xlii 43
   i 26–30 ..... C.R. xvii 467
     132–146 ..... C.R. xiii 432
     140f. ..... C.R. xvii 468
     147–149 ..... ib.   466
     150f. ..... J.P. xxxiv 43
     155f. ..... ib.   45
     166f. ..... C.R. iii 315
     168 ..... J.P. xxxiv 42
   ii 143–148 ..... C.R. xviii 395
   iii 4 ..... C.R. xvii 467
     109 ..... C.P.P. 1904 5
     236f. ..... J.P. xxxiv 40
   vi 58 ..... C.R. xxxiv 163
     329 ..... C.R. xl 170
     365 o 1–34 passim ..... C.R. xiii 266; xv 263;
xvii 393
     7–13 ..... C.R. xviii 397

LUCAN (*cont.*)

vii 303 a–c	C.R. xlvi 150
320–325	C.R. xv 405
380f.	C.Q. xiii 78
460–465	C.Q. xv 172
x 542	C.Q. xvii 166

LUCILIUS

18 Marx	C.Q. i 54
36	ib. 56
40–42	ib. 148
109	ib. 54
130	ib. 148
181–188	ib. 149
258f.	ib. 57
265f.	ib. 59
300f.	ib. 151
334	ib. 65
344f.	ib. 157
352–355	ib. 72
388	ib. 57
450f.	ib. 151
457	ib. 65
484–489	ib. 152
534–536	ib. 66
564	ib. 153
610	ib. 66
631	J.P. xxxii 266
691	C.Q. i 61
700	ib. 154
732	ib. 60
735	ib. 67
948f	ib. 154
1002	ib. 57
1004	C.R. xlix 166

LUCILIUS (*cont.*)

1041f.	c.q. i	155
1043f.	ib.	155
1058	ib.	156
1071f.	ib.	156
1134f.	ib.	157
1344f.	ib.	158
1347	ib.	67

LUCRETIUS

i 312–316	J.P. xxv	226
440–446	ib.	227
490f.	ib.	228
1052–1068	ib.	230
ii 270	ib.	228
456–463	ib.	232
500–503	ib.	234
788–794	ib.	235
936	ib.	228
iii 370f.	c.q. ix	32
522	J.P. xxv	228
717	c.q. iii	63
916–918	J.P. xxv	237
iv 84–89	ib.	238
217–229	ib.	230
1171–1184	ib.	240
v 1261	ib.	239
1262–1268	ib.	241
1308–1315	ib.	242
1341–1349	c.r. xlii	122
1440–1445	J.P. xxv	243
vi 47–49	ib.	245
237	ib.	238
572–574	ib.	246
777–780	ib.	247

LUCRETIUS *(cont.)*

vi 921–9	J.P. xxv 229
962–964	ib. 248
1179–1182	ib. 249

MACROBIUS

ii 3 16	C.R. xxxii 163

MANETHO

279	C.Q. ii 49

MANILIUS

mss of	C.R. xiv 466; C.Q. i 290; xv 175
i passim	J.P. xxvi 60
394	C.R. xli 71
423	C.R. xvii 343
794f.	C.R. xi 289
ii 471–474	C.R. xiv 466
571	ib. 34
iii 271–274	C.R. xx 114
355	C.Q. xvii 166
592–594	C.Q. ii 314
605	ib. 314
608–617	ib. 313
iv 6	C.P.P. 1913 16
53	ib. 17
124	ib. 17
133–135	ib. 17
204	J.P. xxvii 162
502–504	C.Q. vii 111
756f.	C.R. xiv 466
773–777	C.Q. vii 112
882	C.R. xiv 38
v passim	J.P. xxvii 162
44	C.R. xvi 343

MANILIUS (*cont.*)

v	107	c.q. xvii 166
	238–240	j.p. xxx 253
	350–352	c.q. xxiv 12
	404	c.p.p. 1913 17

MARTIAL[1]

spect.	4		j.p. xxx 229
	5		ib. 230
	19	3	c.r. xxxix 201
	21		c.r. xv 154
	21	B	ib. 155; j.p. xxx 230
	27	2	c.r. xxxix 201
	28	9–12	j.p. xxx 231; c.q. xxi 6
i	17		j.p. xxx 232
	42	2	ib. 265
	48	6	c.r. xxxix 202
	68		c.q. xiii 68
	69		j.p. xxx 233
	106	6	c.r. xlv 82
ii	28	6	ib. 82
	36	1–4	j.p. xxx 233
	46	3	ib. 265
	52	2	ib. 234
	64	4	ib. 265
	71	5	ib. 265
	77	1–4	ib. 234
	83		Hermes lxvi 407
iii	13	2	c.r. xxxix 202
	20	1–5	c.q. xiii 69; xvii 163
	42	4	c.r. xxxix 200

[1] Housman contributed some corrections of Martial to J. D. Duff's text in J. P. Postgate's *Corpus*. I have included in this article references to some adversaria by Markland published by Housman in j.p. xxx 265.

MARTIAL *(cont.)*

iii 58	41	J.P. xxx 265
72	2	C.R. xxxix 200
80	1	ib. 202
82	32f.	J.P. xxx 258
93	18–22	ib. 235; C.R. xxii 46
95	11f.	J.P. xxx 235
iv 17		Hermes lxvi 407
58	2	C.R. xxxix 200
67	8	ib. 200
69		J.P. xxx 236
v 7	5	ib. 265
14	1–3	ib. 236
16	5–8	C.Q. xiii 70
19	7–14	J.P. xxx 236
22	7	C.R. xxxix 202
38	7	J.P. xxx 265
66		C.Q. xiii 71
vi 14		ib. 71
21		J.P. xxx 238
25	1–2	ib. 239
29	1f.	ib. 240
	7f.	C.Q. xiii 73
36		Hermes lxvi 409
39		J.P. xxx 240
64	3	C.R. xxxix 202
vii 10	1f.	Hermes lxvi 410
18	1	C.R. xxxix 202
28	10	J.P. xxx 265
34		ib. 241
35	1–6	Hermes lxvi 409
47	6	C.R. xlv 81
49	2	ib. 82
79		J.P. xxx 242; xxxi 42

OVID (*cont.*)

her. ix	153–158	C.R. xi 239
x	29–32	ib. 239
	67–75	ib. 240
	83–86	ib. 241
	110	ib. 428
	145 f.	ib. 241
xi	76	C.R. xiii 174
	121–128	C.R. xi 241
xii	62–66	ib. 286
	89–92	ib. 286
xiii	37–40	C.R. xx 41
	73 ff.	C.R. xi 200; xvi 444
	137 f.	C.R. xiii 176
xiv	53–66	C.R. xi 287
	79–82	ib. 288
	101–108	ib. 288
	125	C.R. xiii 172
xv	39–44	C.R. xi 289
	103 f.	ib. 428
	113	C.Q. x 147
	129	C.R. xi 106
	139 f.	ib. 289
	197 f.	ib. 290
	201 f.	ib. 290
xvi	35–40	ib. 425
	83 f.	ib. 426
	121–123	ib. 427
	277 f.	C.R. xiii 176
xvii	51 f.	C.R. xi 427
xviii	65 f.	ib. 427
	119–22	ib. 427
	187–194	ib. 427
xix	59–62	C.Q. iii 248
	171–174	C.R. xv 405

OVID (*cont.*)

met. vii 741 f.	c.p.t. iii	146
864 f.	ib.	146
viii 237	ib.	147
x 169 f.	ib.	147
202 f.	ib.	148
636 f.	ib.	148
731–733	ib.	149
xi 180 f.	ib.	149
270–272	ib.	150
472	j.p. xvi	35
523	c.p.t. iii	151
xii 24–26	ib.	151
xiii 601–603	ib.	151
724–727	ib.	152
xiv 200	ib.	152
xv 622–625	ib.	152
838	c.q. x	144
fast. iii 793	c.q. ix	33
iv 174	j.p. xxxi	261
v 157 f.	c.r. xx	258
vi 345–347	c.q. xxiv	11
trist.		
codex Holkhamicus	j.p. xxxv	291
i 1 16	c.q. x	130
7 5–8	ib.	130
ii 191 f.	c.q. i	277
275–280	c.q. x	131
iii 2 23 f.	ib. 131; c.p.p. 1927 31	
4 71 f.	c.q. x	133
6 1–8	c.q. ix	37
8 11	c.q. x	133
11 61 f.	ib.	134
14 47–50	ib.	135

PETRONIUS

9	C.R. xviii 398
41 6–8	C.R. xxxii 164
141	J.P. xxxii 265

PHAEDRUS

i 15	C.R. xx 257
iii prol. 20	C.R. xxxiv 122
34–37	C.Q. xiii 69; C.R. xxxiv 124; C.Q. xvii 163
2 5	C.R. xxxiv 123
17 5–11	C.R. xx 258
iv 2 4	C.R. xxxiv 122
9 3–12	C.R. xx 258
17 8	C.R. xxxiv 123
v 10 6	ib. 123
app. Perott. 13 1–5	C.R. xx 259
14 5–8	ib. 259
17	ib. 259
24 2	C.R. xxxiv 124

PINDAR

paeans [P. Ox. v 841] passim	C.R. xxii 8

PLAUTUS

capt. 15	C.Q. ix 230
rud. 766–768	C.R. xxxii 162

PLINY

n.h. xxxv 179	C.Q. xxvii 3

PLINY

paneg. 60 5	J.P. xxx 252
61 1	ib. 252

POETAE LATINI MINORES (Baehrens)
See Anthologia Latina, Cicero, Dracontius, Germanicus, Grattius, Ilias Latina, Nemesianus, Ovid, Priapea, Virgil

PROPERTIUS (*cont.*)

i 8	11–16	J.P. xxii 91
	13	J.P. xvi 2
	17–20	J.P. xxi 169
	22	J.P. xvi 2
	26	J.P. xxi 183
	36	J.P. xxii 101
	45	J.P. xxi 163
9	32	J.P. xvi 2
11	6	ib. 2
	11	J.P. xxii 109; C.R. xlviii 139
	15f.	J.P. xvi 2
	22	ib. 2
	29	J.P. xxi 189
13	12	J.P. xvi 2
15	25f.	ib. 2
	29	ib. 3
	33	ib. 2
16	9	ib. 3
	23	ib. 3
17	3	ib. 3
	28	ib. 3
18	15	ib. 3
	23f.	ib. 3
	27	ib. 3
19	13	ib. 3; xxi 184
	16	J.P. xvi 3
20	3f.	ib. 3
	24	ib. 3, 291
	27	J.P. xxii 110
	30	J.P. xvi 3
	52	ib. 3; xxii 105, 122
21	9	J.P. xxi 184
22	8ff.	J.P. xvi 3

PROPERTIUS (*cont.*)

ii 9 18	J.P. xvi 5
20f.	ib. 5
29f.	ib. 5
44	ib. 5
10 2	ib. 5, 291
11f.	J.P. xxi 186
11 1	ib. 186
12 6	J.P. xvi 5; C.R. xxxvii 121
18	J.P. xxii 111
13 1	J.P. xvi 5; xxi 117
25	C.Q. xxi 10
38	J.P. xvi 5
39f.	ib. 5
45	ib. 5
47	J.P. xxi 139
48	J.P. xvi 5
55	ib. 5
14 5	ib. 5; xxii 85
7f.	J.P. xvi 5
29–32	ib. 5; xxii 85
15 passim	J.P. xvi 5
1	ib. 5
23–26	J.P. xxi 187
31–36	J.P. xvi 4
37	ib. 6
41–48	ib. 8
49	J.P. xxii 93
16 passim	J.P. xvi 6
12	J.P. xxi 172
41f.	J.P. xvi 10
17 passim	ib. 6
11f.	C.R. ix 353
15f.	C.R. xix 320

PROPERTIUS (*cont.*)

ii	25	47	J.P. xxi 119
	26	15	ib. 130
		23	J.P. xvi 7
		28–32	ib. 7
		53	J.P. xxi 188
		54	J.P. xvi 7; xxi 192
	27	7	J.P. xvi 7; xxi 118, 188
		14	J.P. xxi 173
	28	passim	J.P. xvi 7
		9f.	J.P. xxi 131
		40	J.P. xvi 4
		51	ib. 7
		57f.	ib. 8
		61f.	ib. 8, 291
	29	27	ib. 8; c.r. ix 351
		36	J.P. xvi 8; xxii 112
		39	c.q. xxi 9
		41	J.P. xxii 87
	30	passim	J.P. xvi 8
		18ff.	ib. 5
		19	J.P. xxi 154
		21f.	J.P. xvi 3
		35	ib. 8
	31	7	J.P. xxi 189
	32	5f.	J.P. xvi 8; xxi 119
		7f.	J.P. xvi 8
		9	ib. 291
		13	J.P. xxii 94
		15f.	J.P. xvi 8
		25–30	ib. 8
		29	J.P. xxi 189
		32	J.P. xvi 8
		33–36	J.P. xxi 152; c.r. xix 319

PROPERTIUS (*cont.*)

ii	32	37	J.P. xvi 8; xxii 87
		41 f.	J.P. xvi 8
		43–46	ib. 8
		61	ib. 8
	33	2	C.R. xlviii 137
		6	J.P. xvi 8
	34	1 f.	J.P. xxi 164
		12	J.P. xvi 9, 291; xxi 174
		13–16	C.R. ix 351
		29 f.	J.P. xxi 154; C.R. ix 353
		31 f.	J.P. xxi 155
		31–54	J.P. xvi 9
		35 f.	C.R. xiv 259
		40	J.P. xvi 9, 291; xxi 165
		43	J.P. xxi 128
		53	J.P. xxii 88
		59	J.P. xvi 9
		61	ib. 9; xxii 119
		83	J.P. xvi 9; xxi 159
iii	1	1	J.P. xvi 31
		23	J.P. xxi 155
		27	ib. 126
		32	J.P. xvi 291
	2	24	ib. 9; xxii 89
	3	41	J.P. xvi 9
	4	4	ib. 9; xxi 121
		14–18	J.P. xvi 9
	5	9	ib. 9
		11	ib. 9; xxv 244
		15	J.P. xvi 9
		35	J.P. xxi 175
		39	ib. 165; xxxv 307
		40–42	J.P. xvi 9
	6	3–8	ib. 9

PROPERTIUS (*cont.*)

iii 6 9f.		c.r. xix 320
	21f.	j.p. xxi 115; c.r. xlviii 137
	28	j.p. xvi 9, 291; xxi 190
	40	j.p. xvi 9
	41	j.p. xxi 116
	7 passim	j.p. xvi 9
	46	j.p. xxi 156
	60	j.p. xvi 10; xxi 179
	8 12–18	j.p. xvi 10, 291
	19f.	j.p. xxi 116
	35f.	j.p. xvi 10
	9 9	ib. 10; xxi 147
	16	j.p. xvi 10
	25	ib. 10
	33f.	ib. 4; c.q. viii 151
	35	j.p. xxi 160
	37f.	c.r. ix 352
	49–51	j.p. xvi 10
	10 23	ib. 10
	11 13–20	ib. 10
	17	ib. 10
	24	j.p. xxi 191
	25	ib. 157
	34f.	c.r. ix 353
	36–42	j.p. xvi 10
	47–68	ib. 10
	70	ib. 10
	12 25	ib. 10
	81–84	ib. 259
	13 9	ib. 10
	12ff.	ib. 10
	19f.	ib. 11

PROPERTIUS (*cont.*)

iii	22	25	J.P. xvi 12; xxi 176; c.r. xlviii 138
		41	J.P. xvi 12
	23	11	J.P. xxi 158
		14	J.P. xvi 12
		17 f.	ib. 12
	24	9–12	ib. 12
		19	ib. 12
		20	J.P. xxi 189
iv	1	7	J.P. xvi 12
		19	ib. 12; xxii 102
		27 f.	J.P. xxi 132
		28 ff.	J.P. xvi 12, 15
		31 f.	J.P. xxi 122
		31–56	J.P. xvi 12
		31	ib. 13
		33–36	ib. 15
		50	ib. 13
		57–70	ib. 13
		81 f.	ib. 13
		85–88	ib. 13
		119	J.P. xviii 15
		120	J.P. xvi 13
		124	ib. 13, 34; c.q. vii 25
		135	J.P. xvi 26
		140–144	ib. 13
	2	passim	ib. 13
		1 f.	J.P. xxi 123
		2	J.P. xvi 13
		12	ib. 13, 291
		19	J.P. xxi 192
		34	ib. 193
		35	J.P. xvi 13

PROPERTIUS (*cont.*)

iv 2 39	J.P. xvi 13	
43 f.	ib. 133	
58	J.P. xxii 120	
3 7–10	J.P. xvi 13; xxi 161	
8	J.P. xxii 95	
11	J.P. xvi 13; xxi 148	
29–62	J.P. xvi 13	
48	ib. 14	
51 f.	J.P. xxi 128	
62	J.P. xvi 14	
63	ib. 14	
4 1	ib. 12	
15	ib. 12	
17 f.	ib. 14	
47	ib. 14	
55	J.P. xxii 90	
57	J.P. xxi 167	
64	J.P. xxii 113	
71 f.	J.P. xvi 14; xxi 177	
82	J.P. xvi 14	
83	ib. 291	
86 ff.	ib. 14	
87	ib. 14	
5 14	C.R. xlviii 138	
19 f.	J.P. xvi 14; xxii 103	
21	J.P. xvi 14; xxi 124	
29–62	J.P. xvi 14	
35 f.	J.P. xxi 141	
57 f.	ib. 159	
64	C.Q. xxi 5	
6 21	C.R. xlviii 138	
22	J.P. xxi 193	
26	J.P. xvi 14; xxii 107	
33 ff.	J.P. xvi 11	

PROPERTIUS (*cont.*)

iv 6	34 ff.	J.P. xvi 14
	45–52	ib. 14
	49	ib. 14
	81	ib. 14
7	4	ib. 14; C.R. ix 355
	7	J.P. xxi 178
	15	ib. 189
	20	ib. 167
	23	J.P. xvi 14, 291
	40–42	J.P. xxi 134
	55–58	J.P. xvi 15
	64	ib. 15
8	1	ib. 15
	4	ib. 15
	9–12	ib. 15
	13	ib. 291
	38	J.P. xxi 178
	39	J.P. xvi 15
	52 ff.	ib. 15
9	21	ib. 15
	29	ib. 15
	31	ib. 15
	40	J.P. xxi 178
	45	ib. 194
	60	J.P. xvi 15
	70	ib. 15
10	19	C.R. v 295
	19–22	J.P. xvi 15
	23–26	ib. 15
	31	C.R. xxxix 203
	37	J.P. xvi 15
	41 f.	J.P. xxi 117
	43 f.	C.R. ix 352
11	passim	J.P. xvi 16

PROPERTIUS (*cont.*)

iv 11 8	J.P. xxi 179
15	J.P. xvi 16
30	J.P. xxii 108
40	J.P. xvi 16
50	ib. 16
70	J.P. xxii 90
87	J.P. xvi 16
101 f.	J.P. xxi 194; C.R. ix 351

SALLUST

| *Iug.* 93 2 | C.Q. xvii 165 |

SENECA

Ag.	726–733	C.Q. xvii 169
Herc. fur.	21	J.P. xvi 35
	154–157	C.R. xiv 259
	448–458	C.Q. xvii 164
	766 f.	C.P.T. iii 140
	1191	C.Q. xvii 171
Herc. Oet.	42–45	C.R. xx 45
	322	C.Q. xvii 171
	335–338	C.R. xv 405
	1170–1176	C.Q. xvii 163
	1176–1186	ib. 170
	1219	C.R. v 295
	1512–1514	C.Q. iii 248
	1608	C.Q. xvii 166
	1696–1704	ib. 171
	1840	ib. 171
	1852	ib. 171
Med.	652–669	ib. 166
Oed.	952–956	ib. 169
Phaedr.	617–619	C.P.T. iii 150

SENECA (*cont.*)

Phaedr.	989 f.	c.q. xvii	167
	1201–1212	ib.	168
Phoen.	8	ib.	171
Thy.	976–979	ib.	170
Tro.	52	c.q. xiii 78	
	386–390	c.q. xvii	165
	766–770	ib.	163
	1120–1126	ib.	165
Oct.	806–810	ib.	171
	964	ib.	172
apocol.	3	c.q. vii 20	
nat. quaest. i	16 7	Hermes lxvi 405	
	vii 31 3	c.r. xviii 398	
epist.	108 32	j.p. xxxii 262	

SILIUS

ii	59 f.	j.p. xxxv 309
xiii	798–802	c.q. ix 32; j.p. xxxv 287

SOPHOCLES

Ai.	784 f.	j.p. xx 33
	795–802	ib. 33
	957	a.j.p. xiii 142
	1100	j.p. xx 48
	1310–1313	ib. 48
	1393–1399	ib. 35
El.	17–19	c.r. ii 244
	453–460	j.p. xx 36
	475	ib. 48
	537–541	ib. 37
	564	c.r. i 240
	708–711	j.p. xx 38
	800 f.	ib. 48
	838	j.p. xvi 275
	841	j.p. xx 48

SOPHOCLES (*cont.*)

El.	930f.	J.P. xx 39
	1327	ib. 48
	1394	ib. 48
	1466f.	ib. 41
Oed. tyr.	216–218	ib. 29
	420–423	ib. 47
	430	C.R. xxxix 77
	596–598	J.P. xx 30
	602	ib. 47
	685	ib. 47
	794–796	C.R. xxxix 79, 214
	866f.	J.P. xx 47
	876	ib. 47
	1031	ib. 47
	1134	A.J.P. xiii 160
	1219	C.R. xxxix 79
	1242f.	J.P. xx 47
	1275–1279	ib. 31
	1349–1351	ib. 32
	1382f.	ib. 47
	1494f.	ib. 47
	1505f.	ib. 47
Ant.	69f.	ib. 25
	126	C.R. xxxix 79
	437–440	J.P. xx 26
	548	ib. 27
	578f.	ib. 34
	746	ib. 28
	1019–1022	ib. 28
	1240f.	J.P. xvi 248
Trach.	141–146	J.P. xx 42
	232–235	ib. 43
	256	ib. 48
	575–577	ib. 44

SOPHOCLES (*cont.*)

Trach.	910f.	C.R. xxxix 78
Phil.	83–85	J.P. xx 48
	348f.	ib. 44
	424f.	ib. 45
	606–609	ib. 45
	761	ib. 48
	984f.	ib. 46; C.R. xxxix 78
	1048	J.P. xx 48
	1407	C.R. xxxix 78
	1443f.	J.P. xx 48
Oed. Col.	131	A.J.P. xiii 156
	263–269	ib. 139
	357–360	ib. 146
	380f.	C.R. xxxix 78
	478–481	A.J.P. xiii 149
	515f.	ib. 150
	527f.	ib. 151; C.R. vii 449
	534f.	C.R. xxxix 80
	720f.	A.J.P. xiii 152
	755–760	ib. 153; C.R. xxii 12
	811–815	A.J.P. xiii 154
	887–890	ib. 155
	978–981	ib. 156
	1016–1038	ib. 157
	1132–1136	ib. 162
	1201–1205	ib. 163
	1249–1253	ib. 164
	1354–1359	ib. 164
	1472–1474	ib. 165
	1510–1515	ib. 166
	1744–1747	ib. 168

II. SUBJECTS

130

INDEX

[1] The classification follows Manilius i, pp. liv ff.

132

manuscripts, errors of (*cont.*)

inversion of three letters with alteration (Greek)	J.P. xvi 262
inversion of three letters with alteration (Latin)	J.P. xviii 17; xxv 249
inversion of four letters (Latin)	J.P. xviii 17
inversion of four letters with alteration (Latin)	ib. 18
rearrangement of four or more letters (Greek)	J.P. xx 30
rearrangement of four or more letters (Latin)	J.P. x 191; xviii 14; C.Q. x 144
transposition of two letters across an intervening space (Latin)	J.P. xviii 31; C.R. xi 103
transposition of syllables (Greek)	C.R. i 240; J.P. xx 42
transposition of syllables (Latin)	C.P.T. iii 146; C.R. iii 201; J.P. xxx 229; C.Q. ix 37
transposition of verses	C.Q. viii 155; J.P. xxxiv 228
transposition of words	J.P. xviii 6, 10, 25
uester and *noster* confused	C.R. viii 253
word taken from next line	C.Q. x 141
March, beginning of year	C.Q. xxvi 131
Martial, persons addressed in	C.Q. xiii 79
mas, uir 'manhood'	C.Q. vii 28, Hermes lxvi 405
mergere	C.R. xxix 174
metre and prosody	
astronomical poets, position in	C.Q. ii 50, 54
choriambus and ditrochaeus in dactylo-epitrite rhythm	C.R. xii 216
classical metres in English	C.R. xiii 317
dēesse, prāeire, dēire	C.P.P. 1911 12
elision in 5th half-foot of pentameter	C.Q. xxi 6

orthography

orthography (*cont.*)

sacxum, ucxor et sim.	C.R. V 293; J.P. XX 149
Statius, antique spelling in mss of	C.R. XX 37
succipere	J.P. xxi 143
Syracŭsius	C.P.P. 1927 31
Thessalicus, -ius	C.Q. xxviii 127
u = v	J.P. xxi 118
-us = -*ovs*	C.Q. xiii 70; xxiv 12

palaeography, sphere of, in textual criticism	Class. Ass. Proc. xviii 67
παμονή	J.P. xvi 274
planets in astrology	C.Q. ix 34
pleonasm (*mare pelago premit arua* et sim.)	C.Q. xxvii 4
pluperfect indic. for pert. and imperf.	C.R. xix 317; J.P. xxi 189; Class. Ass. Proc. xviii 82

Polluris	C.Q. xii 30
preposition, misleading position of	J.P. xxv 247
preposition with second of two nouns	C.R. xvii 304; C.Q. X 149
punicus, -eus	J.P. xxxv 309

-*que* attached to -*ĕ*	J.P. xxi 151
qui = quisquis, quicunque	C.Q. xxviii 132
quis interrogative and exclamatory	C.R. xx 41; C.Q. xvii 170; xxvii 14
quīs, quibus	C.Q. xvii 171
quo) (cur	C.Q. X 132

retiarii, costume of	C.R. xviii 397
retorridus, meaning of	J.P. xxxii 267
reuincere, meaning of	C.R. xi 103

securicella	C.P.P. 1916 12